The SPIRIT with Our SPIRIT

WITNESS LEE

Living Stream Ministry

Anaheim, California • www.lsm.org

First Edition, September 1994.

ISBN 978-0-87083-798-2

Published by

Living Stream Ministry
2431 W. La Palma Ave., Anaheim, CA 92801 U.S.A.
P. O. Box 2121, Anaheim, CA 92814 U.S.A.

Printed in the United States of America

11   12   13   14   15   16   /   12   11   10   9   8   7   6   5

CONTENTS

Title   *Page*

Preface   5

1 The Meaning of the Word *Spirit* in the Bible
   and the Basic Revelation concerning God
   and Man in the Holy Scriptures   7

2 The Definition of the Spirit (1)   17

3 The Definition of the Spirit (2)   27

4 The Definition of the Spirit (3)   37

5 The Definition of the Spirit (4)   49

6 The Definition of Our Spirit   59

7 The Importance of Our Human Spirit   69

8 The Exercise of Our Spirit   77

9 The Spirit's Work on and in the Believers (1)   87

10 The Spirit's Work on and in the Believers (2)   97

11 The Spirit's Work on and in the Believers (3)   107

12 The Spirit's Work on and in the Believers (4)   117

13 The Spirit's Work on and in the Believers (5)   127

14 The Spirit's Work on and in the Believers (6)   137

PREFACE

This book is composed of messages given by Brother Witness Lee in Anaheim, California from August 28 through December 17, 1993.

CHAPTER ONE

THE MEANING OF THE WORD *SPIRIT* IN THE BIBLE AND THE BASIC REVELATION CONCERNING GOD AND MAN IN THE HOLY SCRIPTURES

Scripture Reading: Ezek. 37:1, 5, 9; John 3:5-6; Rev. 11:11; John 3:8; 4:24; Gen. 1:2b; Matt. 28:19b; John 14:10-11, 26; 15:26; 10:30; 8:29, 16b; 16:32b; Acts 10:38; Luke 4:1a, 18a; Gen. 2:7; Prov. 20:27; Zech. 12:1; Isa. 42:5; Job 32:8; Heb. 4:12; 1 Thes. 5:23a; John 4:24; 1 John 4:13; 2 Tim. 4:22a; 1 Cor. 6:17

OUTLINE

Note: The general subject is not "The Spirit *and* Our Spirit" but "The Spirit *with* Our Spirit."

I. The meaning of the word *spirit* in the Bible:
   A. The Hebrew equivalent of the word *spirit* is RUACH, denoting:
      1. Spirit—Ezek. 37:1.
      2. Breath—Ezek. 37:5.
      3. Wind—Ezek. 37:9.
   B. The Greek equivalent of the word *spirit* is PNEUMA, denoting:
      1. Spirit—John 3:5-6.
      2. Breath—Rev. 11:11.
      3. Wind—John 3:8.
II. The basic revelation concerning God and man in the Holy Scriptures:
   A. Concerning God:
      1. "God is Spirit," denoting God's essence, substance—John 4:24.

2. "The Spirit of God," denoting that the Spirit is God—Gen. 1:2b.

3. "The name of the Father and of the Son and of the Holy Spirit," denoting the Divine Trinity and indicating that God is triune—Matt. 28:19b:

   a. The three of the Divine Trinity coexist and coinhere as one God—John 14:10-11, 26; 15:26; 10:30.

   b. They are distinct but not separate—John 8:29, 16b; 16:32b; Acts 10:38; Luke 4:1a, 18a.

B. Concerning man:

1. Created by God as a tripartite man—Gen. 2:7:

   a. With a body formed with the dust of the ground, as man's outer frame.

   b. With a spirit produced of the breath of God (the same Hebrew word for "breath" in Genesis 2:7 is translated into "spirit" in Proverbs 20:27), as man's inmost organ.

   c. With a soul, the issue of God's breath breathed into the nostrils of the body formed of dust, as man's inner being (person).

2. The spirit of man was created by God, in a particular sense, to complete God's purpose in the creation of the heavens and the earth—Zech. 12:1; Isa. 42:5; Job 32:8.

3. Man's spirit is distinct from his soul—Heb. 4:12; 1 Thes. 5:23a.

C. God is Spirit for man to contact Him and receive Him into man, and man has a spirit for man to contact God and contain God that God and man may have an organic union—John 4:24; 1 John 4:13; 2 Tim. 4:22a; 1 Cor. 6:17.

In this series of messages, we are still on the general subject of the Christian life. In order for us to experience the Christian life, we surely need to know God, the Lord, Christ, as the Spirit. Also, we have to know that for us to enjoy this Spirit, we have a spirit within us.

From my youth I have loved the Bible, and I have studied it for years. I have found that we can study the Bible in two ways. One way is to study it according to the letter and another way is to study it in the Spirit. Paul said, "The letter kills, but the Spirit gives life" (2 Cor. 3:6). We want to know the Lord's word, not just by the letter but by the Spirit. The unique writer of the Bible is the Spirit (2 Pet. 1:21; 2 Sam. 23:2). Throughout the years we have released many messages on the Spirit as the consummation of the Triune God. But we have the burden once again to see the Christian life from its very foundation, and the foundation of the Christian life is the Spirit with our spirit.

The general subject of this series of messages is not "The Spirit *and* Our Spirit" but "The Spirit *with* Our Spirit." We do not use the conjunction *and* but the preposition *with*. Romans 8:16 says, "The Spirit Himself witnesses *with* our spirit." *With* is a preposition, and it is instrumental. If we say the Spirit *and* our spirit, this is a compound subject. Our spirit is not the subject and should not be the subject. Our spirit is the helper. If I do things *with* you, you are not the subject but the instrument. You are my helper. Our spirit is not the subject. The subject must be the Spirit.

I. THE MEANING OF THE WORD
SPIRIT IN THE BIBLE

A. The Hebrew Equivalent
of the Word *Spirit* Is *Ruach*,
Denoting Spirit, Breath, or Wind

In Ezekiel 37 the Hebrew word *ruach* is used to refer to the Spirit (v. 1), breath (v. 5), and wind (v. 9). The way in which *ruach* is translated depends on the context of the sentence or paragraph.

B. The Greek Equivalent of the Word *Spirit* Is *Pneuma,* Denoting Spirit, Breath, or Wind

In the New Testament, the Greek word *pneuma* may be translated also as Spirit (John 3:5-6), breath (Rev. 11:11), or wind (John 3:8). We know that *pneuma* is the wind in John 3:8 because "the wind blows." Revelation 11:11 also uses *pneuma* when speaking of the resurrection of the two martyred witnesses. It says "the breath [*pneuma*] of life out of God entered into them." Some translate this as "the Spirit of life." Second Thessalonians 2:8 says that the Lord will slay Antichrist, the lawless one, "by the breath of His mouth." The word *breath* here is also the Greek word *pneuma.*

II. THE BASIC REVELATION CONCERNING GOD AND MAN IN THE HOLY SCRIPTURES

The Bible is a book on both God and man. We need to see the basic revelation concerning God and man in the Holy Scriptures.

A. Concerning God:

1. "God Is Spirit," *Denoting God's Essence, Substance*

John 4:24 says that "God is Spirit." Saying that God is Spirit is similar to saying that a chair is wood. Wood refers to the essence, the substance, of the chair. Thus, *God is Spirit* does not refer to the person of God but denotes God's essence, substance. This was spoken by the Lord in John 4 to the Samaritan woman concerning the worship of God. In order to worship God, we have to realize that the One whom we are worshiping is Spirit in essence, in substance.

2. "The Spirit of God," *Denoting That the Spirit Is God*

The Spirit of God denotes that the Spirit is God (Gen. 1:2b). Phrases like *the Spirit of God, the light of God,* and *the life of God* are in apposition. This means that the Spirit is God, the light is God, and the life is God. In God's creation, the creating God was the moving Spirit. Without being the

Spirit, God could not do anything and would not do anything. He does everything as the Spirit. In the Bible, God's move in every step is the Spirit's moving.

3. *"The Name of the Father and of the Son and of the Holy Spirit," Denoting the Divine Trinity and Indicating That God Is Triune*

Matthew 28:19 says that we need to go and baptize people "into the name of the Father and of the Son and of the Holy Spirit." *The name of the Father and of the Son and of the Holy Spirit* denotes the Divine Trinity and indicates that God is triune. He is one God yet three—the Father, the Son, and the Spirit.

a. The Three of the Divine Trinity Coexist and Coinhere as One God

The three of the Divine Trinity coexist and coinhere as one God from eternity to eternity (John 14:10-11, 26; 15:26; 10:30). Hence, He is the eternal God (Psa. 90:1-2). To coexist is to exist together at the same time. To coinhere is to mutually indwell one another. The Father exists in the Son and the Spirit; the Son exists in the Father and the Spirit; and the Spirit exists in the Father and the Son. This is coinherence. In John 14, the Lord Jesus Himself told us that He is in the Father and the Father is in Him (vv. 10-11). The Lord also said that when He came from the Father, He came with the Father (John 8:16, 29; 16:32b). This means that when He comes, the Father comes in Him. Christ comes with the Father, and the Spirit comes with Christ (John 14:26; 15:26). The three are coinhering. The Lord Jesus also revealed that His speaking is the Father's working (John 14:10). Thus, the Son's speaking is the Father's working, and the Spirit's moving is the Son's moving and the Father's moving. The three do not only coexist but also coinhere.

b. They Are Distinct but Not Separate

The three of the Godhead are distinct, but not separate (John 8:29, 16b; 16:32b; Acts 10:38; Luke 4:1a, 18a). Since They are coinhering, They cannot be separated. They coexist by the way of coinhering. But there is still a distinction among

Them. The Father is the Father, the Son is the Son, and the Spirit is the Spirit. These three titles denote that They are distinct. But when the Son speaks, that is the Father's working. When the Spirit comes, that is really the coming of the Father and of the Son. Thus, They are one, with distinction but no separation.

What I have presented here is the most simple and brief way to speak on the Divine Trinity. What is our God? He is Spirit. Who is the Spirit? The Spirit is God. Who are the Father, the Son, and the Spirit? The Father, the Son, and the Spirit are the Divine Trinity. They are distinctly three but not separate. They are still one. They do not only coexist but also coinhere as one yet three.

According to the economical aspect of the Trinity, the Father planned, the Son accomplished, and the Spirit applies to us what the Son has accomplished according to the Father's plan. The Father accomplished the first step of His plan, His economy, by working to choose and predestinate us, but He did this in Christ the Son and with the Spirit (Eph. 1:3-5). After this plan was made, the Son came to accomplish this plan, but He did this with the Father (John 8:29; 16:32) and by the Spirit (Luke 1:35; Matt. 1:18, 20; 12:28). After the Son accomplished all that the Father had planned, the Spirit comes in the third step to apply all that He accomplished, but He does this as the Son and with the Father (John 14:26; 15:26; 1 Cor. 15:45b; 2 Cor. 3:17). In this way, while the divine economy of the Divine Trinity is being carried out, the divine existence of the Divine Trinity, His eternal coexistence and coinherence, remains intact and is not jeopardized. In the divine economy, the three work and are manifested respectively in three consecutive stages. Yet even in Their economical works and manifestations, the three still remain essentially in Their coexistence and coinherence.

B. Concerning Man

1. Created by God as a Tripartite Man

It is very meaningful that God is triune and man is tripartite. God is in three persons—the Father, the Son, and the

Spirit—and we men are tripartite, in three parts—the spirit, the soul, and the body. Man was created by God as a tripartite man (Gen. 2:7).

a. With a Body Formed with the Dust of the Ground, as Man's Outer Frame

Genesis 2:7 says that the Lord formed man of the dust of the ground. Our body is our outer frame formed with the dust of the ground.

b. With a Spirit Produced of the Breath of God (the Same Hebrew Word for "Breath" in Genesis 2:7 Is Translated into "Spirit" in Proverbs 20:27), as Man's Inmost Organ

Man was created by God with a spirit produced of the breath of God, as man's inmost organ. I use the word *produced* here because the origin of our spirit is the breath of life. The Hebrew word for "breath" in Genesis 2:7 and for "spirit" in Proverbs 20:27 is not *ruach* but *neshamah*. Proverbs 20:27 says, "The spirit [*neshamah*] of man is the lamp of Jehovah" (ASV). Our body is the frame and this frame has an organ, our spirit. This is the highest organ within us and is mainly for us to contact God. John 4:24 says that God is Spirit and they who worship Him must worship in spirit. We must worship God in our spirit as an organ to contact Him.

c. With a Soul, the Issue of God's Breath Breathed into the Nostrils of the Body Formed of Dust, as Man's Inner Being (Person)

When God's breath was breathed into the nostrils of man's body formed of dust, there was an issue. This issue was the soul of man as man's inner being (person). We have only one person, and our person is the soul. There are a number of times when the Bible says "souls" when speaking of persons. Exodus 1:5 speaks of the seventy souls that came out of Jacob. These were the seventy persons of the house of Jacob who went down to Egypt. The New Testament also refers to persons as souls (Acts 27:37). Our soul is our person. The outer frame is our body, the inner being is our soul, and the inmost organ is our spirit. You have a frame, you are a person, and this person in the frame has an organ, which is mostly for contacting God.

2. The Spirit of Man Was Created by God, in a Particular Sense, to Complete God's Purpose in the Creation of the Heavens and the Earth

The spirit of man was created by God, in a particular sense, to complete God's purpose in the creation of the heavens and the earth (Zech. 12:1; Isa. 42:5; Job 32:8). Zechariah 12:1 says that God stretched forth the heavens, laid the foundation of the earth, and formed the spirit of man within him. Zechariah put these three things together: the heavens, the earth, and the spirit of man. The heavens are for the earth, the earth is for man, and man has a spirit for God. Thus, man is the center of God's creation, and the center of man is his spirit.

Without the heavens to give sunshine, air, and rain, the earth could not grow anything, and we could not live. All the living things—plants, animals, and man—need sunshine, air, and rain. Otherwise, they will die. Thus, the heavens are for the earth. Also, the earth was created for the existence of man, and man has a spirit within him to contain God. We are living on the earth with the supply from the heavens for the purpose of being one with God. God created an organ within us for this purpose.

The record in Genesis 1 and 2 tells us about God's creation. It says God created the heavens and then the earth with the plant life and animal life. But when the record comes to the creation of man, it gives us a particular point. This point is that within man, God created a spirit out of His breath of life. This is something particular in the completion of God's purpose in the creation of the heavens and the earth. God created the heavens and the earth because He wants to have man as His expression. In order for man to be God's expression, this man needs a spirit to contact God and to contain God. God created the heavens for the earth, God created the earth for man, and God created a spirit for man so that man can contact Him to be one with Him organically.

3. Man's Spirit Is Distinct from His Soul

The Bible reveals that man's spirit is distinct from his soul (Heb. 4:12; 1 Thes. 5:23a). Our experience also tells us this. According to our mind, we may feel to buy something. We may really like it and desire to have it according to our emotion. Then we may decide to get it according to our will. Thus, our mind thinks about it in a good way, our emotion loves it, and our will determines to get it. At this juncture, however, there is something else deep within that tells us not to get it. This is our spirit, the deepest and inmost part of our being. This is the distinction between the soul and the spirit.

The highest part, the high peak, the highlight, of a man is the spirit. The lowest part, the meanest part, is the body. In between, in the middle, is the soul. If you live by your body, you become a low person. If you live by your spirit, you become the highest person, a person of the highest grade. Or you may be in the middle. You may be quite logical, knowledgeable, and reasonable. This is to live according to your soul. You are neither low nor high; you are in the middle.

If you live by the body, you live like a beast. If you live by the spirit, you are a genuine saint. Every believer should be a saint who lives by the spirit. But if you live by the soul, you are merely a gentleman, like a disciple of Confucius. You are very logical, reasonable, and full of knowledge. A gentleman is a logical and reasonable man. When you lose your temper without limitation by the desire and lust of the flesh, of the body, you are like a beast. When you are losing your temper and restrict it by your logic and reason, you are a gentleman in the soul. When you restrict your temper by exercising the spirit, you are a saint.

C. God Is Spirit for Man
to Contact Him and Receive Him

God is Spirit for man to contact Him and receive Him into man, and man has a spirit for man to contact God and contain God that God and man may have an organic union (John 4:24; 1 John 4:13; 2 Tim. 4:22a; 1 Cor. 6:17). If God were not the Spirit, He could not contact us, and we could not contact Him.

God the Father is the source; God the Son is the course; and God the Spirit is the flow to reach us (2 Cor. 13:14). Thus, the Spirit is the reaching of the Divine Trinity to man. God reaches us in the Son as the Spirit. Ephesians 2:18 says, "For through Him we both have access in one Spirit unto the Father." The Spirit is the access for us to contact God, receive God, and contain God.

This is so that we and God may have an organic union. Our union with God is not like the union in today's American labor unions. That union is in an organizational and coexisting way, but our union with God is organic. It is a union not only of coexistence but also of coinherence. Today we are coinhering with God. He lives in us, and we live in Him. In John 15 the Lord said, "Abide in Me and I in you" (v. 4a). First John 4:15 and 16 speak of God abiding in us and us in God. This is a mutual abiding, and this mutual abiding is coinherence. It is only after being regenerated to have God in us as our life and nature that we are in union with God organically. This union is a coinherence, a mutual abiding. This is the Bible's revelation concerning God and man. We all have to know Him and know ourselves to such an extent.

The exercise of the spirit
does not always release
the spirit. The release ministers
others—we have to push out our spirit
To release our spirit requires us
to not care for our face. The spirit
has to pass through our soul.

*even our sinning can
effect our unity.

CHAPTER TWO

THE DEFINITION OF THE SPIRIT

(1)

Scripture Reading: Gen. 1:2; Judg. 3:10; 6:34; Gen. 6:3a; Psa.
51:11; Isa. 63:10-11; Luke 1:13-17, 30-36; Matt. 1:18-20; Mark
1:10, 12; Matt. 4:1; Luke 4:1, 18; John 1:32-33; 7:37-39; 1 Cor.
15:45b; Rev. 21:6; 22:17c

OUTLINE

O.T. the power
f Holy Spirit
is seperate
but in the N.T.
is just the power
Spirit but the
essence.

I. In the Old Testament the Spirit is:
   A. The Spirit of God in God's creation of the universe—
      Gen. 1:2. but the Spirit of God (Elohim) was brooding
   B. The Spirit of Jehovah in God's reaching of men
      and in His care for men—Judg. 3:10; 6:34; Gen.
      6:3a. → God's reaching & caring for men
      striving (intimacy)

seperates
man
into mingle
w/ man

   C. The Spirit of holiness in God's making His chosen   The separate
      people holy unto Himself—Psa. 51:11; Isa. 63:10-11.   God's ppl

II. In the New Testament the Spirit is: Luke 1:15²
    A. The Holy Spirit: divine power but of   The Holy Spirit =
                              divine essence   The Spirit the holy

the diff. btwen
IA+B. this msg is on
the definition of the Spirit.
& need to know who the
Spirit is. How was the
Spirit involved @ the
very beginning.

       1. In the conception of John the Baptist to   God's
          introduce God's becoming a man in His incarna-   miracle that
          tion—Luke 1:13-17.   power & essence   involved the
                                                     divine essence
                                                     power

       2. In the conception of Jesus in God's incarnation   & God's
          to be a man in the flesh—Luke 1:30-36; Matt.   miracle that
          1:18-20.   God was incarnated   w/ divine power & essence   God's incarna-
                      in the flesh   added to man   tion.

    B. The Spirit:
       1. With whom Jesus was anointed and who was in
          the move of the man Jesus in His ministry to
          God on the earth—Mark 1:10, 12; Matt. 4:1;
          Luke 4:1, 18; John 1:32-33. Matt 3:16²⁻⁹ Heb 10:19-20²
                                          Matt 3:17¹
                                          Matt 3:22¹
                                          Luke

2. But in the believers to flow out as rivers of
living water was not yet before Christ's glorification—resurrection—John 7:37-39.

3. Through and in His resurrection Christ as the
last Adam became the life-giving Spirit to enter
into His believers to flow out as rivers of living
water—1 Cor. 15:45b; Rev. 21:6; 22:17c.

Spirit class prep.

1. In God's creation the Spirit was the Spirit of God (Gen 1:2) After God's creation God began
to work on man as Jehovah so the Spirit of Jehovah refers to God's reaching of men, &
His care for men. Jehovah means "clean" so the one who works on man is everything
to man. God is caring for man to make them holy so we have the Spirit of
holiness who is working to seperate God's ppl to Himself.

2. The Spirit the Holy means that He is the Holy to not only make man seperated unto
Him but also one w/ Him. Eventually the Spirit the Holy is 7-fold intensified in
Rev.

3. With John the Baptist conception the essence of the Holy Spirit was in volved but not
but the power was. However w/ Jesus His conception involved both the divine
power & essence. In Matt 1:20 it speaks of the Holy Spirit begetting
the Lord

The Bible is a book written not only by the Spirit but also with the Spirit (2 Pet. 1:21; 2 Sam. 23:2). God's move in man is altogether a story of the Spirit. Without the Spirit, there is no history of God because God is totally a matter of Spirit. The difference between God's move, God's act, God's work, and religions is that religions do not have the Spirit. They may have some spirits, but those spirits are demonic, devilish, and satanic. There is only one genuine, divine Spirit; that is God Himself. In this message we want to begin to study the definition of the Spirit.

I. IN THE OLD TESTAMENT THE SPIRIT IS:

In the Old Testament, the Spirit is the Spirit of God, the Spirit of Jehovah, and the Spirit of holiness.

A. The Spirit of God
in God's Creation of the Universe

Every story in the Old Testament is related to God. The first story is concerning God's creation of the heavens and the earth, with millions of items, and His creation of man. In this story the Spirit of God is mentioned. Genesis 1:1 says that in the beginning God created the heavens and the earth. Then the following verse says, "The Spirit of God brooded over the face of the waters" (Heb.). Thus, we see that the Spirit was the Spirit of God in God's creation of the universe. In creation God's name according to the Hebrew was *Elohim,* the mighty One and the faithful One.

B. The Spirit of Jehovah
in God's Reaching
of Men and in His Care for Men

After His creation, God began to work on man. In God's work on man, His name is *Jehovah.* The Spirit of Jehovah is in God's reaching of men and in His care for men (Judg. 3:10; 6:34; Gen. 6:3a). The title *Jehovah* literally means "He that is who He is"; therefore, "the eternal I Am." As Jehovah, He is the One who was in the past, who is in the present, and who is to come in the future (Rev. 1:4). *Jehovah* simply means *to be.* God was, God is, and God shall be forever. He is the great I Am.

God told Moses that His name was "I Am That I Am" (Exo. 3:14). This means, "I am always the thing which should be." If there is a need of light, He is the light. If there is a need of life, He is the life. He is everything. The Lord Jesus Himself told us that His name is "I Am" (John 8:58). The name *I Am* means that the very One who works on man is everything to man. He takes care of man and He comes upon man. This is *Jehovah* in His reaching of man and in His care for man.

C. The Spirit of Holiness
in God's Making His Chosen People Holy
unto Himself

God is caring for man mainly to make man holy. To be holy means to be separated unto God. Man's fall caused him to depart from God to become common, worldly, secular, and even dirty. So God needs to take care of man, making man separate from all things other than Himself. This is to make man holy. Thus, the Spirit in the Old Testament is the Spirit of holiness in God's making His chosen people holy unto Himself (Psa. 51:11; Isa. 63:10-11). This is not the same as *the Holy Spirit,* which is used in the New Testament. The Holy Spirit is more intensified than the Spirit of holiness.

II. IN THE NEW TESTAMENT THE SPIRIT IS:

Now we come to the New Testament. In the New Testament, the revelation concerning the Spirit is more complicated.

A. The Holy Spirit

The first divine title used for the Spirit in the New Testament is *the Holy Spirit.* According to the Greek text, the title translated as *the Holy Spirit* may be in two forms: *the Spirit the Holy* or *the Holy Spirit.* According to my understanding, this means that in the New Testament age, the very God who is the Spirit is "the Holy." God is a Spirit and this Spirit now is totally "the Holy." We are now in an age in which God Himself as the Spirit is "the Holy" to make man not only separated unto Him but also one with Him. In the

Old Testament, the most God could do with man was to make man separated unto Him but not one with Him. But now in the New Testament age, the time has come in which God would go further and deeper to make man absolutely one with Him, to make man Him and to make Him man. Athanasius, who was one of the church fathers, said concerning Christ: "He was made man that we might be made God." This means that we are made God in life and in nature, but not in the Godhead. This process takes place by *the Spirit the Holy.*

In the New Testament, two divine titles of the Spirit are very striking: the first one and the last one. The first one is *the Spirit the Holy* and the last one is *the seven Spirits* (Rev. 1:4; 4:5; 5:6). *The Spirit the Holy* is for making man God, making man one with God and making God one with man. In other words, the New Testament age is for bringing God and man together, to constitute them together so that they coinhere (mutually indwell each other) to be one spirit (1 Cor. 6:17). Man and God become one spirit, one entity. Eventually, *the Spirit the Holy* has to be seven times intensified to become the seven eyes of the Lamb. All the living creatures were made by God with two eyes, but eventually the Lamb will have seven eyes, and these seven eyes are the seven Spirits of God, the sevenfold-intensified Spirit.

1. In the Conception of John the Baptist to Introduce God's Becoming a Man in His Incarnation

In the Old Testament, *the Spirit of holiness* is mentioned but not *the Holy Spirit. The Holy Spirit* is applied first to John the Baptist. This title is used in the conception of John the Baptist to introduce God's becoming a man in His incarnation (Luke 1:13-17). Luke 1:15 says concerning John the Baptist, "He will be filled with the Holy Spirit, even from his mother's womb." The preparing of the way for the Savior's coming required that His forerunner, John the Baptist, be filled with the Holy Spirit even from his mother's womb, so that he could separate the people unto God from all things other than God, making them holy unto Him for His purpose. Luke 1:15*

2. In the Conception of Jesus in God's Incarnation to Be a Man in the Flesh

The beginning of the New Testament gives us a record of two conceptions. One was the conception of John the Baptist and the other was the conception of the Lord Jesus in God's incarnation to be a man in the flesh (Luke 1:30-36; Matt. 1:18-20). With these two conceptions, the New Testament uses the particular title *the Holy Spirit*. *The Holy Spirit* is used in the New Testament due to the change of the age. In order for God to become a man so that man could become God, there was the need of the Holy Spirit. The Old Testament was an age of figures and types, but the New Testament is the time of fulfillment, the age of reality, in which God became a man by being begotten of the Holy Spirit into humanity (Matt. 1:18, 20).

We need to see that the conception of John the Baptist was strikingly different in essence from that of Jesus the Savior. With John's conception, the essence of the Holy Spirit was not involved but the power. The conception of John was by the power of the Holy Spirit through man's instrument. But with the conception of Jesus, the very essence of the Holy Spirit Himself was involved. Thus, Matthew 1:20 says concerning the begetting of Jesus in Mary, "That which has been begotten in her is of the Holy Spirit." The conception of John the Baptist was God's miracle, accomplished with the human essence, merely by the divine power without the involvement of the divine essence. This resulted in the bringing forth of a mere man who was filled with the Spirit of God but who lacked the nature of God. The conception of the Savior was God's incarnation (John 1:14), constituted not only by the divine power but also of the divine essence added to the human essence, thus producing the God-man of two natures—divinity and humanity. These two conceptions are related to the beginning of God making Himself man and of God making man Him that He might become man and man might become Him, that the two could be one entity.

B. The Spirit:

1. With Whom Jesus Was Anointed and Who Was in the Move of the Man Jesus in His Ministry to God on the Earth

The Spirit anointed Jesus and was in the move of the man Jesus in His ministry to God on the earth (Mark 1:10,12; Matt. 4:1; Luke 4:1, 18; John 1:32-33). After Jesus was baptized, the Spirit as a dove descended upon Him. In symbolic form, Jesus is the Lamb, and the Spirit is the dove. The Spirit as the dove came upon Jesus as the Lamb to carry out God's redemption and salvation for the accomplishing of God's economy.

Luke 4 says that the coming down of the dove upon the man Jesus was the anointing (vv. 1, 18). Jesus was anointed with the Spirit as a dove. This anointing made Jesus a particular man. In the Old Testament, a number of people were anointed with oil, and then the Spirit came down to reach the anointed one (Exo. 29:7; 1 Sam. 9:16; 16:12; 1 Kings 1:34; 19:15-16). But the anointed one was not anointed with the Spirit directly. In the New Testament, however, Jesus was anointed directly with the Spirit as a dove.

This anointing Spirit is not referred to as *the Spirit of Jehovah* or as *the Spirit of God* but simply as *the Spirit*. The reality and the essence of God's statuses in the Old Testament are implied in *the Spirit*. This means that this anointing Spirit was in God's status as the Creator and in His status as the One who was, who is, and who is to be. In the Old Testament the Spirit is God, the Spirit is Jehovah, and the Spirit is holiness. Jesus was anointed with such a Spirit who is God, who is Jehovah, and who is holiness.

After the baptism of Jesus, we see Him standing in the water, the Spirit coming down upon Him, and the Father speaking from the heavens. This is a picture of the Divine Trinity. The Father is in the heavens, the Son is on the earth in the water, and the Spirit is in the air. They are in three locations. This is mentioned in the first three, synoptic Gospels, Matthew, Mark, and Luke (Matt. 3:16-17; Mark 1:9-11; Luke 3:21-22). These Gospels deal mainly with the Lord's humanity.

But the fourth Gospel, the Gospel of John, deals mainly with the divinity of the Son of God. John shows that the three of the Divine Trinity are one. John 14:26 says that the Father sends the Spirit in the Son's name. But John 15:26 says that the Son sends the Spirit from the Father. The sense in the Greek for the word *from* here is actually *from with*. These verses indicate that the Father and the Son are one. They both sent the Spirit. Then when the Spirit came from the Father, He came with the Father. The Son also said that He was never alone, because the Father was always with Him (John 8:29; 16:32). This is mainly concerning His divinity.

The synoptic Gospels are mainly concerned with Christ's humanity. In these Gospels we see that God, Jehovah, who is the very holiness, came down upon the man Jesus as the Spirit to be one with this man. The anointing God is one with the anointed man. The dove was in the air. The Lamb was on the earth. But now here is one entity—the dove on the Lamb. The One in the air is now one with the One on the earth. God and man have become one, indicating a kind of organic union. The anointing Spirit and the man Jesus became one in His ministry. The Spirit was not only for the anointing of the man Jesus but also for the move of the man Jesus in His ministry to God for three and a half years on this earth.

2. The Spirit within the Believers, Flowing Out as Rivers of Living Water, Was Not Yet

The Spirit was there to anoint Christ and to move with Christ, but at that time the Spirit had not yet entered into the believers to flow out as rivers of living water (John 7:37-39). In this sense "the Spirit was not yet." John 7 tells us that the Spirit was not yet, because by that time Jesus was not glorified in His resurrection. Resurrection was for the man Jesus to get out of His human shell and to release the divine life, and this resurrection is called glorification. Before Christ was thus glorified, the Spirit was not yet. When John said "the Spirit was not yet," he meant that the Spirit was not yet to flow out of the believers as rivers of living water. But the Spirit was there for the anointing of Christ and the moving of Christ in His ministry.

The anointing of Jesus the man and the moving with Jesus the man was God making Himself one with man on a small scale in an individual way, with one person. But when the Spirit flows into the believers and flows out of them as many rivers of living water, God being one with man and man being one with God becomes a corporate matter. It is not just with one man, Jesus, but with millions of His believers. This is the enlargement of God being one with man. God's being one with man altogether depends upon the Spirit. The Spirit is a big key to the organic union of God with man.

3. Through and in His Resurrection Christ as the Last Adam Became the Life-giving Spirit to Enter into His Believers to Flow Out as Rivers of Living Water

Through and in His resurrection Christ as the last Adam became the life-giving Spirit to enter into His believers to flow out as rivers of living water (1 Cor. 15:45b; Rev. 21:6; 22:17c). God is a Spirit and the second of the Triune God in the flesh became a life-giving Spirit. Prior to Christ's resurrection, God was a Spirit but not a life-giving Spirit. Before Christ's death and resurrection, God had no way to enter into man to be man's life. Between man and God there were a number of negative things as obstacles. According to the typology seen in Genesis, the way to God as the tree of life was closed by the requirements of God's glory, God's holiness, and God's righteousness (Gen. 3:24; see *Life-study of Genesis,* pp. 282-286). A fallen, sinful, unclean man was altogether unable to take the tree of life, to take God in as life, until Christ's death fulfilled these requirements.

Hebrews 10 reveals that the death of Christ opened the way, a new and living way, so that we can go into the Holy of Holies to partake of God as the tree of life (vv. 19-20). In His death He fulfilled all the requirements of God's glory, holiness, and righteousness; then in resurrection He changed in form to be the life-giving Spirit. This was absolutely for the organic union between God and man—to bring God into man and to bring man into God in His resurrection. Today we can take the tree of life and drink the water of life so that the Triune God can flow out from our innermost being as rivers of living water.

CHAPTER THREE

Hymns 539

THE DEFINITION OF THE SPIRIT

(2)

Scripture Reading: 1 Cor. 15:45b; Rev. 21:6; 22:17c; Acts 16:7; Rom. 8:9b; Phil. 1:19b; 2 Cor. 3:17-18; Rom. 12:2b; 1 Cor. 3:6, 9b, 12a; Eph. 4:16b; Matt. 28:19b; John 14:16-17; 15:26b; 16:13; 1 John 5:6b; Eph. 2:18; 2 Cor. 13:14

Eg. point requires a lot of X.

OUTLINE

II. In the New Testament the Spirit is:

   B. The Spirit: *a J to memory & verses*

     3. Through and in His resurrection Christ as the last Adam became the life-giving Spirit to enter into His believers to flow out as rivers of living water—1 Cor. 15:45b; Rev. 21:6; 22:17c:

       a. The Spirit of Jesus concerning Jesus in His humanity, who passed through human living and death on the cross, indicating that in the Spirit there is not only the divine element of God but also the human element of Jesus and the elements of His human living and of His suffering of death as well—Acts 16:7.

       b. The Spirit of Christ concerning Christ in His divinity, who conquered death and became the life in resurrection with the resurrection power, indicating that in the Spirit there is the element of divinity that became the death-conquering and life-dispensing Spirit—Rom. 8:9b.

c. The Spirit of Jesus Christ, comprising all the elements of Jesus' humanity with His death and Christ's divinity with His resurrection, which become the bountiful supply of the unsearchable Christ for the support of His believers—Phil. 1:19b.

d. The Lord Spirit, the pneumatic Christ—2 Cor. 3:17-18:

   1) For the metabolic transformation of the believers into the Lord's image, from glory to glory.

   2) By the renewing of the mind—Rom. 12:2b.

   3) For the growth and the building up of the Body of Christ—1 Cor. 3:6, 9b, 12a; Eph. 4:16b.

e. To consummate the processed Triune God—Matt. 28:19b:

   1) As the Father, the Son, and the Holy Spirit.

   2) Consummating in the last of the Divine Trinity, that is, the Holy Spirit, as the consummation of the processed Triune God.

f. To be the Paraclete, the Comforter, to the believers—John 14:16-17.

g. To be the reality of the processed Triune God—John 14:17a; 15:26b; 16:13; 1 John 5:6b.

h. To be the reaching of the processed Triune God to the believers.

i. To be the believers' access unto the Father, the source of the Divine Trinity—Eph. 2:18.

j. To be the fellowship of the processed Triune God with the believers for their enjoyment of the riches of the Divine Trinity—2 Cor. 13:14.

Handwritten margin notes:

f: This comforter is the Sp of Reality is w/us forever & abides w/us. It is Jesus. This comforter is Ølimited by the flesh. This is an eternal marriage.

when we pray (sisters) we give our case to our advocate. We can't defend ourselves. He takes care of our case by interceding for us.

Our relationship w/ the Father is unconditional but our fellowship our peace w/ the Father is conditional.

we have to believe
that when he forgives us
releases us. He died for us
when we were His enemy
would He condemn us

←This is a family affair.. O thing 2 d o w/ Satan!

Jesus
did.

THE DEFINITION OF THE SPIRIT   29

We have seen that John 7:39 says, "The Spirit was not yet." It is difficult to explain why John 7:39 says this. We saw that Jesus was anointed with the Spirit and that the Spirit was in the move of the man Jesus in His ministry to God in His last three and a half years on the earth. Furthermore, the Lord Jesus told the disciples that they would be filled with the Spirit and that the Spirit would flow out of them as rivers of living water. Then John tells us that at that time, the Spirit was not yet, because Jesus was not yet glorified. The Spirit of God was there from the beginning, but at the time the Lord spoke this word, the Spirit as the Spirit of Christ (Rom. 8:9), the Spirit of Jesus Christ (Phil. 1:19), was not yet, because the Lord had not yet been glorified.

For Jesus to be glorified was for Him to be resurrected (Luke 24:26). Before Christ was resurrected, the Spirit who would flow into the believers and flow out of them as rivers of living water was not yet. His being glorified may be likened to the blossoming of a flower. When the flower blossoms, that is its glorification. Jesus was glorified in resurrection. The Spirit flowing into and out of the believers as rivers of living water would not come into being until after Jesus' resurrection. It was through the resurrection and after the resurrection of Jesus, that the Spirit became the life-giving Spirit (1 Cor. 15:45b) to enter into the believers and flow out of them as rivers of living water.

We have seen that in the Old Testament, the Spirit was the Spirit of God in God's creation of the universe, the Spirit of Jehovah in God's reaching of men and in His care for men, and the Spirit of holiness in God's making His chosen people holy unto Himself. Now we come to the New Testament, which is much more important than the Old Testament.

In the New Testament, the Spirit was firstly the Holy Spirit in two conceptions: the conception of John the Baptist, the forerunner of Christ, and the conception of Christ, which was God being born into humanity. The very God who entered into the womb of Mary was the Holy Spirit. So Matthew 1:20 says that what was born in the womb of Mary was of the Holy Spirit. This was much different from God's creation, from God's relationship with man, and from God's making His people holy. This is God as the Holy One, "the Spirit the Holy," entering into a human virgin to be born there. God was born into man. God Himself as the Holy One entered into a human virgin and stayed in her womb for nine months. Then a child came out who was named Jesus. Isaiah 9:6 says that this child is called the mighty God and the eternal Father. God was born into the womb of Mary, and Jesus was born out of Mary to be the child who is called the mighty God as the Creator in His creation and the eternal Father as the source of all the positive things.

At the end of the previous message, we pointed out that through and in His resurrection Christ as the last Adam became the life-giving Spirit to enter into His believers to flow out as rivers of living water. *The last Adam* means the conclusion of humanity, the ending of humanity. There were only two Adams: the first Adam and the last Adam. The first Adam is the beginning of humanity, and the last Adam is the ending of humanity. First, we were a part of the first Adam, but now we are a part of the last Adam.

We need to see the revelation of the Bible in an intrinsic way. Let us consider the example of a big tree. There is a flowing, a current, within this big tree. That is the juice of that tree. The tree's story does not depend upon its outward frame, but it depends upon its intrinsic flow, its intrinsic current. The Bible is the divine revelation composed of sixty-six books. There are many things covered in this book, but what is the intrinsic flow of the Bible? The intrinsic flow of the Bible is the Spirit.

The Spirit began to flow from Genesis 1:2. Right after God came to create, the Spirit began to move. That is the beginning of the very current of the Bible through its entire sixty-six books. This current is consummated in Revelation 22:17, which speaks of "the Spirit." Thus, the flow of the Spirit began in Genesis 1:2 and will consummate in Revelation 22:17. In between these two ends of the Bible is a long current. This long current is the history of God's move among man and within man. The history of God among man and within man is a current of the flow of the Spirit. The definition of the Spirit includes the entire history of God's move among man and within man. If we see this, we will understand the Bible intrinsically and get the real significance of the Bible.

Now the Spirit has become the life-giving Spirit. This life-giving Spirit is a wonderful One who came into being through two "becomings." The first becoming was God becoming a man (John 1:14). He became the last Adam, and was called by the name *Jesus*. Then this man became the life-giving Spirit (1 Cor. 15:45b). These are two big events in human history and also in God's history. In the history of the entire universe, nothing could be bigger than God's incarnation. That was God becoming a man. Then after thirty-three and a half years this man became something else. He was God, He became a man, and this man became a life-giving Spirit.

a. The Spirit of Jesus

In the New Testament, the life-giving Spirit is referred to as *the Spirit of Jesus* (Acts 16:7). This title of the Spirit is concerning Jesus in His humanity, who passed through human living and death on the cross. It indicates that in the Spirit there is not only the divine element of God but also the human element of Jesus and the elements of His human living and suffering of death.

b. The Spirit of Christ

The Spirit of Christ is concerning Christ in His divinity, who conquered death and became the life in resurrection with the resurrection power, indicating that in the Spirit there is the element of divinity that became the death-conquering and the life-dispensing Spirit (Rom. 8:9b).

c. The Spirit of Jesus Christ

The Spirit of Jesus Christ refers to the Spirit, comprising all the elements of Jesus' humanity with His death and Christ's divinity with His resurrection, who becomes the bountiful supply of the unsearchable Christ for the support of His believers (Phil. 1:19b).

d. The Lord Spirit, the Pneumatic Christ

The Lord Spirit is a compound title (2 Cor. 3:18) referring to the pneumatic Christ. This is similar to the compound title *the Father God*. This does not mean that the Father and God are separately two. The Father and God are one. *The pneumatic Christ* refers to Christ as the Spirit. Christ and the Spirit are not separately two; They are one. The Lord Spirit is the pneumatic Christ.

The Lord Spirit, the pneumatic Christ, is for the metabolic transformation of the believers into the Lord's image, from one degree of glory to a higher degree of glory (2 Cor. 3:17-18). Such transformation takes place by the renewing of the mind (Rom. 12:2b), and this is for the growth and the building up of the Body of Christ (1 Cor. 3:6, 9b, 12a; Eph. 4:16b).

e. To Consummate the Processed Triune God

1) As the Father, the Son, and the Holy Spirit

There are many hints in the Old Testament through which we can know that God is triune, but it is difficult to see in the Old Testament that the Triune God is the Father, the Son, and the Holy Spirit. It is not until the end of the first Gospel in the New Testament that we see the composition of the Divine Trinity (Matt. 28:19b). The composition of the Father, of the Son, and of the Holy Spirit was not clearly and completely unveiled until after Christ's resurrection. After His resurrection, and before His ascension, He came back to the disciples and charged them to disciple the nations, baptizing them, the new believers, into the name of the Father and of the Son and of the Holy Spirit. In the Acts the apostles baptized people into the name of Jesus Christ (8:16; 19:5). This means that Jesus Christ equals the Father, the Son, and the Spirit. Before the man Jesus became the life-giving Spirit, the Divine Trinity was not fully consummated.

The Second of the Divine Trinity is the Son. He is the only begotten Son of God (John 3:16) and the firstborn Son of God (Rom. 8:29). Before Christ was incarnated, He did not have humanity; before His incarnation the Son was only divine.

Furthermore, before His resurrection the Son was God's only begotten Son, not the Firstborn. In this sense, the Second of the Divine Trinity was not fully consummated before His resurrection. He needed to pick up humanity through incarnation, and He needed to become the firstborn Son of God through resurrection (Acts 13:33). So after His incarnation and resurrection, the Second of the Trinity was completed, consummated.

Now we need to consider the Third of the Divine Trinity—the Spirit. Before the incarnation and resurrection, the Spirit was only the Spirit of God, not the Spirit of Man. The Spirit of Jesus is the Spirit of Man. In the Spirit of God prior to the incarnation, there was no human living, no all-inclusive death, and no element of resurrection. In other words, before the incarnation and the resurrection, the Spirit of God was not compounded. It was through incarnation, human living, crucifixion, and resurrection that the Spirit of God was compounded with humanity and with Christ's death and resurrection. So after Christ's resurrection, the Third of the Divine Trinity was also consummated. After the resurrection, the Spirit of God is the life-giving Spirit, the Spirit of Jesus, the Spirit of Christ, the Spirit of Jesus Christ, and the Lord Spirit. All these aspects of the Spirit are for the consummation of the Triune God. The Triune God was consummated in Christ's resurrection, so after His resurrection the Lord came back to say that we are to baptize people into the name of the Father and of the Son and of the Holy Spirit.

2) Consummating in the Last of the Divine Trinity, That Is, the Holy Spirit, as the Consummation of the Processed Triune God

The Triune God has been consummated in the life-giving Spirit, the Spirit of Jesus, the Spirit of Christ, the Spirit of Jesus Christ, and the Lord Spirit. So this Spirit today is the consummation of the Triune God.

f. To Be the Paraclete, the Comforter, to the Believers

The Spirit as the consummation of the processed Triune God is the Paraclete, the Comforter, to the believers (John

14:16-17). In John 14:16 the Lord said He would ask
the Father to give us another Comforter. The Comforter is the
Paraclete. The Greek word here means "advocate, one alongside who takes care of our cause, our affairs." The Spirit who
is the life-giving Spirit, the Spirit of Jesus, the Spirit of
Christ, the Spirit of Jesus Christ, and the Lord Spirit is the
Paraclete to us, the One who is always alongside of us to take
care of our case, our affairs, and our needs.

g. To Be the Reality of the Processed Triune God

The life-giving Spirit is the reality of the processed Triune
God (John 14:17a; 15:26b; 16:13; 1 John 5:6b). If we have this
Spirit, we have the reality of the Divine Trinity, who is pro-
cessed and consummated.

h. To Be the Reaching of
the Processed Triune God to the Believers

The life-giving Spirit is the reaching of the processed
Triune God to the believers. If there were not such a Spirit,
the Triune God would have no way to reach us. The Father is
the source; the Son is the course; and the Spirit is the reaching. The Triune God reaches us through the Spirit that gives
life.

i. To Be the Believers' Access unto the Father,
the Source of the Divine Trinity

The Spirit is also the believers' access unto the Father
(Eph. 2:18), the source of the Divine Trinity. For the Spirit to
be the "reaching" means that He comes to us. For Him to be
the "access" means that we go to Him. This is the proper com-
munication—coming and going. This Spirit is God's coming,
and this Spirit is also our entrance, the access. Without the
Spirit, there is no entry, no access, for us to enter into
the Triune God. For the Triune God to reach us, we need the
Spirit. For us to enter into the Triune God, we need the Spirit.
This Spirit is God's reaching; He is also our entry, our access,
into the Divine Trinity.

j. To Be the Fellowship of the Processed Triune God with the Believers for Their Enjoyment of the Riches of the Divine Trinity

Second Corinthians 13:14 reveals that the Spirit is the fellowship of the processed Triune God with the believers for their enjoyment of the riches of the Divine Trinity. When He reaches us, and we enter into Him, there is the fellowship. Then we remain in the fellowship to enjoy all the riches of the Triune God embodied in Christ.

Study Questions

1. The intrinsic flow of the Bible is the Spirit. In Gen 1:2 after God created the Spirit began to move + this move continued throughout the entire Bible until Rev 22:17 which speaks of "the Spirit". Throughout the Bible we the Spirit + His among man + in man

2. Before incarnation + resurrection the Sp was only the Sp of God + of man. However after the Lord went through this process the Spirit of G. was compounded w/ humanity, X death + resurrection. Now the Spirit of G. is the life-giving Sp. the Sp. of Jesus, the Sp of X, the Sp of Jesus X, + the Lord Sp. all of these are for consummation of the 3-1 G. And now this life-giving Sp. is the reality of the processed 3-1 G. as we have this Sp. we have the reality of the Divine Trinity

3. Personal experience of God's reaching

This oil is a full type of the spirit ^anointing

3 & 5 are R/t God's building ??

= means creature
= unique God

we need to see the vision of the compound ointment if we don't see this then our experience of the c. spirit will be uplifted & continuous.

The Lord is dwelling place = tabernacle a priesthood - those experiencing Him & being satisfaction to Him to allow Him as the anointing in us to move in us & out of us.

[Is exodus 15:7-16:6]

The context of the rev. of the c. ointment is the tabernacle & priesthood.

we are both His dwelling place & His priesthood.

CHAPTER FOUR

THE DEFINITION OF THE SPIRIT

(3)

myrrh, cinnamon calamus, cassia, & olive oil = anointing oil

And you have an anointing from the holy one, & all of you know

Scripture Reading: Exo. 30:22-30; 2 Cor. 1:21; 1 John 2:20, 27;
Eph. 1:13, 11, 14; 4:30b; 2 Cor. 1:22; Gal. 3:8, 14; John 3:5-6;
Heb. 2:10; Gal. 4:6; Rom. 8:14-16; 15:16; 8:26; Titus 3:5b; 2 Cor.
5:17

We need to exercise our spirit w/our speaking

The stimulation of our vision & His death which is in the sp.

OUTLINE

8 aspects that need 2 b brought unto us

II. In the New Testament the Spirit is:

C. The compound anointing Spirit—Exo. 30:22-30:

The more you take care of your spirit the more you take care of & enter into the reality of the oneness

1. Compounded with the unique God, as the base, as the divinity of Christ, typified by the one hin of olive oil—v. 24b.

2. With God's Divine Trinity, typified by the three units of five hundred shekels of the spices—vv. 23-24a.

3. With Christ's humanity, typified by the four kinds of spices. *every x we touch the spirit we touch the humanity of Jesus & every aspect of*

4. With Christ's death and its killing effective-ness, typified by (myrrh) and (cinnamon)—v. 23a. *His humanity express divinity*

5. With Christ's resurrection and its repelling power, typified by (calamus) and (cassia)—vv. 23b-24a.

6. As an ointment for the anointing of all the things and persons related to the worship of God—vv. 25-30; (2 Cor. 1:21;) 1 John 2:20, 27.

7. As the Holy Spirit to seal the believers of Christ—Eph. 1:13; 4:30b; 2 Cor. 1:22a:

      a. To dispense the divine element of the pro-
cessed Triune God into the believers and
saturate them with it.

      b. Transforming the believers into the inheri-
tance of God—Eph. 1:11.

    8. As the sealing Spirit to be a pledge to the
believers—Eph. 1:14; 2 Cor. 1:22b:

      a. Guaranteeing God as the inheritance of the
believers.

      b. Giving the believers a foretaste of God as
their heritage.

D. The blessing of the gospel—Gal. 3:8, 14:

greatest miracle of the whole universe →

    1. To regenerate the believers, begetting them as
the many sons of God—John 3:5-6; Heb. 2:10.

    2. As the Spirit of the Son to cry "Abba, Father" in
the believers' heart and to lead the believers to
walk as the sons of God—Gal. 4:6; Rom.
8:14-16.

    3. As the Spirit for the priesthood of the gospel to
sanctify the believers—Rom. 15:16.

    4. To intercede for the believers—Rom. 8:26.

    5. To renew the believers, making them the new
creation of God—Titus 3:5b; 2 Cor. 5:17.

In the previous two messages we have seen that the Lord Jesus had the divine Spirit in Him for His incarnation, human living, and ministry, but at that time He had not yet become the life-giving Spirit (1 Cor. 15:45b) to flow out of His believers as rivers of living water (John 7:38-39). In order for the Spirit to come into the believers and flow out of them, the Lord had to take two more steps. First, He had to die. Second, He had to resurrect. In His death He cleared away the obstacles of sin, the flesh, the world, and Satan so that we could receive the Spirit for the Spirit to flow out of us. Then in His resurrection He became a life-giving Spirit (1 Cor. 15:45b). After the Lord's crucifixion and resurrection, the Spirit can enter into the believers to regenerate them and flow out of them as rivers of living water.

The Spirit eventually became the consummation of the processed Triune God. In the Old Testament, the Spirit was the Spirit of God, the Spirit of Jehovah, and the Spirit of holiness. *The Holy Spirit* is the first title used for the Spirit of God in the New Testament. The birth of Christ was directly of the Holy Spirit. His source was the Holy Spirit and His element was divine.

The thirty-three and a half years from Christ's incarnation to His ascension was a transitory time. Before this transitory time began, before Christ's incarnation, God was purely God. He was merely divine. But the Bible shows us that God intended to enter into man. For Him to enter into man, He needed to become a man. Before that time, He was eternally perfect, complete, but not yet perfected, completed. He was unprocessed, "raw," "uncooked." In those thirty-three and a half years, He passed through the processes of incarnation, human living, crucifixion, resurrection, and ascension. These are the five steps through which the "raw" God passed to become the "cooked" God. It was after this that He sat down in the heavens and became the consummated Triune God.

Before His incarnation, He did not have the human element. He did not have the experience of human living or human suffering. After He created man, He remained separately

from man for four thousand years. But one day He became a
man to bring Himself into humanity. Matthew 1:20 says,
"That which has been begotten in her is of the Holy Spirit."
That means God was born, begotten, into Mary and remained
in her womb for nine months. Then He was born out of that
womb to become a God-man. From that time God and man
became one. But this is not the consummation; this is the
beginning of the process. He grew up as a young man and
passed through human living. Then at the age of thirty, He
came out to be baptized. He worked for God and ministered
God to man for three and a half years. Then He entered into
His crucifixion and was buried in a tomb for three days. He
visited Hades and came out of that region of death into resurrection. Then in resurrection He became the life-giving
Spirit.

Also, in resurrection He was begotten to be the firstborn
Son of God (Acts 13:33; Rom. 8:29). As the only begotten Son
of God (John 3:16), He had merely divinity, not humanity. But
as the firstborn Son of God, He has the elements of humanity,
human living, crucifixion, and resurrection. In resurrection
He became the life-giving Spirit, and He was also begotten to
be the firstborn Son of God. His being the firstborn Son
implies that there are other sons to follow Him. In resurrection He begot us to be the many sons of God. In such a
condition and status, He ascended. Before He came down
from the heavens in incarnation, He was purely God. But He
went back into ascension as a God-man with the elements of
humanity, human living, crucifixion, and resurrection. Now
the Triune God is completed, consummated, "cooked." He has
become the life-giving Spirit, who is the consummation of the
processed Triune God. The processed Triune God today in His
consummation is the Spirit.

In the previous message we saw that this consummated
Spirit who is the consummation of the Triune God is five
things to us. He is the Paraclete, the reality, the reaching, the
access, and the fellowship. As the Paraclete, He is always with
us, going along with us and living in us to be our everything.
This One is the reality. Without this One, God is not real,
Christ is not real, righteousness is not real, holiness is not

real, life is not real, light is not real, and love is not real. The
Spirit as the consummation of the processed Triune God is
the unique reality in the entire universe. Who is God? He
is God. Who is Christ? He is Christ. Who is the Savior? He is
the Savior. Who is the Redeemer? He is the Redeemer. Who
is the Lord? He is the Lord. Who is the Master? He is the
Master. Who is the Father? He is the Father. He is the reality.
First John 5:6b says, "The Spirit is the reality." When He
comes to us, He is the reaching of God to us. Also, He brings
us back to God, and this is our access. Then as we remain in
Him, He is our fellowship.

We need to know the Spirit in such a detailed way. If we do
not know the Spirit thoroughly, we cannot have a proper,
normal Christian life. The normal Christian life depends
upon our knowing and experiencing the Spirit.

C. The Compound Anointing Spirit

Now we want to see a further aspect of the Spirit in the
New Testament. The Spirit is the compound anointing Spirit
typified by the compound ointment in Exodus 30:22-30. Oil is
purely one element, but an ointment is a compound. Paint is a
good example of a compound of oil with a number of elements.
Today in the New Testament the Spirit is the compounded
Spirit to be the anointing ointment.

Brother Watchman Nee taught us that in order to experience Christ's death in Romans 6, we must enter into the
experience of the Spirit in Romans 8. We can experience
Christ's death only in the Spirit. But in his earlier ministry,
he told us that to experience Christ's death, we have to reckon
ourselves dead. That was based upon Romans 6:11. Later, he
found out that reckoning does not work. Reckoning was
stressed by A. B. Simpson, the founder of Christian and
Missionary Alliance. Without the Spirit, however, reckoning
does not work. The more you reckon yourself to be dead, the
more you are alive. The death of Christ is in the Spirit.
Brother Nee also taught us that the reality of resurrection is
the Spirit.

Later, I read Andrew Murray's book *The Spirit of Christ.*
I heard Brother Nee say twice that if anyone would translate

that book into Chinese, he would pay for the printing costs. Around 1951 some of my helpers translated it, and I polished it. So today we have the Chinese translation of *The Spirit of Christ*. One of the most striking chapters in this book is chapter five, entitled "The Spirit of the Glorified Jesus." I would like us to take note of the following parts of this chapter so that we can be impressed with the divine revelation of the Spirit in the New Testament. We have underlined certain parts of the text for emphasis.

> We know how the Son, who had from eternity been with the Father, entered upon a new stage of existence when He became flesh. When He returned to Heaven, He was still the same only-begotten Son of God, and yet not altogether the same. For He was now also, as Son of Man, the first-begotten from the dead, clothed with that glorified humanity which He had perfected and sanctified for Himself. And just so the Spirit of God as poured out at Pentecost was indeed something new. ... When poured out at Pentecost, He came as the Spirit of the glorified Jesus, the Spirit of the Incarnate, crucified, and exalted Christ, the bearer and communicator to us, not of the life of God as such, but of that life as it had been interwoven into human nature in the person of Christ Jesus. It is in this capacity specially that He bears the name of Holy Spirit, for it is as the Indwelling One that God is Holy. ... Christ came...to bring human nature itself again into the fellowship of the Divine life to make us partakers of the Divine nature. ... In His own person, having become flesh, He had to sanctify the flesh, and make it a meet and willing receptacle for the indwelling of the Spirit of God. ...From His nature, as it was glorified in the resurrection and ascension, His Spirit came forth as the Spirit of His human life, glorified into the union with the Divine, to make us partakers of all that He had personally wrought out and acquired,

of Himself and His glorified life. In virtue of His
atonement, man now had a right and title to the
fulness of the Divine Spirit, and to His indwelling, as never before. And in virtue of His having
perfected in Himself a new holy human nature on
our behalf, He could now communicate what pre-
viously had no existence—a life at once human and
Divine. ... In our place, and on our behalf, as man
and the Head of man, He was admitted into the full
glory of the Divine, and His human nature constituted the receptacle and the dispenser of the Divine
Spirit. And the Holy Spirit could come down as
the Spirit of the God-man—most really the Spirit
of God, and yet as truly the spirit of man....Just as
in Jesus the perfect union of God and man had
been effected and finally completed when He sat
down upon the throne, and He so entered on a
new stage of existence, a glory hitherto unknown,
so too, now, a new era has commenced in the life
and the work of the Spirit. He can now come down
to witness of the perfect union of the Divine and
the human, and in becoming our life, to make us
partakers of it. *There is now* the Spirit of the glorified Jesus: He hath poured Him forth; we have
received Him to stream into us, to stream through
us, and to stream forth from us in rivers of blessing.

Andrew Murray's writing on the Spirit of Christ is marvelous. He pointed out that the Spirit of the glorified Jesus has
His human nature. No doubt, the Spirit always had the divine
nature, but in Christ's resurrection, the glorified human
nature along with the elements of human living, crucifixion,
and resurrection were added to the Spirit, who is now the
consummation of the processed Triune God. When I studied
what Andrew Murray said concerning the Spirit of Christ, I
was strengthened, confirmed, and assured to speak on the
all-inclusive Spirit of Christ. I have been speaking on this
wonderful truth for almost forty years.

1. Compounded with the Unique God, as the Base

The best type of the all-inclusive Spirit of Christ as the compound anointing Spirit is the compound ointment spoken of in Exodus 30 (see *Life-study of Exodus,* Messages 157-166, pp. 1679-1776). This type reveals that the compound anointing Spirit is compounded with the unique God, as the base, as the divinity of Christ, typified by the one hin of olive oil (v. 24b).

2. With God's Divine Trinity

The compound anointing Spirit is compounded with God's Divine Trinity, typified by the three units of five hundred shekels of the spices (vv. 23-24a). The middle unit of five hundred shekels was split into two units of two hundred fifty shekels each. This signifies that the Second of the Divine Trinity was split, crucified, on the cross.

3. With Christ's Humanity

The compound anointing Spirit is also compounded with Christ's humanity, typified by the four kinds of spices.

4. With Christ's Death and Its Killing Effectiveness

The Spirit is compounded with Christ's death and its killing effectiveness, typified by myrrh and cinnamon (v. 23a).

5. With Christ's Resurrection and Its Repelling Power

Christ's resurrection and its repelling power, typified by calamus and cassia (vv. 23b-24a), are also elements of the compound anointing Spirit. Calamus is a reed shooting up into the air out of a marsh or a muddy place. Thus, it signifies the rising up of the Lord Jesus from the place of death. Cassia in ancient times was used as a repellent to drive away insects and snakes. Thus, it signifies the repelling power of Christ's resurrection.

6. As an Ointment for Anointing

All the above elements compounded together create an ointment for the anointing of all the things and persons related to
the worship of God (vv. 25-30; 2 Cor. 1:21; 1 John 2:20, 27).

7. As the Holy Spirit to Seal the Believers
of Christ

In the New Testament, we see the compound anointing
Spirit operating as the Holy Spirit to seal the believers of
Christ (Eph. 1:13; 4:30b; 2 Cor. 1:22a). To seal means to
anoint. When a person puts his seal on something, that sealing is the anointing. The Spirit is a living seal that saturates
us with the divine element. We have to pray, "Lord, don't just
seal me once, but saturate me all the time. I need Your sealing; I need Your saturating." When we live by the Spirit, we
have the sense that something within us is saturating us, and
that saturating is the continuous sealing. This sealing dis-
penses the divine element of the processed Triune God
into the believers and saturates them with it. It also transforms the believers into the inheritance of God (Eph. 1:11). It
is remarkable that we sinners can be transformed to such an
extent that we are considered by God as His inheritance. How
could we, the constitution of sin, be God's inheritance? Surely,
this implies transformation.

Our being God's inheritance, as spoken of in Ephesians
1:11, is related to Christ's redemption (v. 7). We were lost in
sin, but Christ's redemption brought us out of sin and unto
God. Then we became persons in Christ. Christ has become
our sphere and our realm in which His element is always saturating us, and that saturating is the Spirit's sealing to
transform us into God's treasure. Today, in Christ, God con-
siders us as His treasure to become His inheritance. The
life-giving Spirit anoints us, seals us, saturates us, with the
divine element. This saturating is the dispensing, and the dispensing is transforming us, making us the treasure of God. If
we walk in the Spirit every day, even every moment, we are
under this sealing, this saturating, to transform us into a
treasure for God's inheritance.

8. As the Sealing Spirit
to Be a Pledge to the Believers

The sealing Spirit becomes a pledge to the believers (Eph. 1:14; 2 Cor. 1:22b), guaranteeing God as the inheritance of the believers and giving the believers a foretaste of God as their heritage. We are God's inheritance, and God is our inheritance. For us to be God's inheritance, we need the sealing. For us to have God as our inheritance, we need the pledging. In ancient times the Greek word for *pledge* was used in the purchasing of land. The seller gave the purchaser some soil from the land as a sample. Hence, a pledge, according to ancient Greek usage, is also a sample. The Holy Spirit is a sample of what we will inherit of God in full.

D. The Blessing of the Gospel

In the New Testament, the Spirit is also revealed as the blessing of the gospel (Gal. 3:8, 14). The blessing of the gospel is the Spirit, the consummation of the Triune God. Nothing is greater than the consummated Triune God.

1. To Regenerate the Believers

The Spirit regenerates the believers, begetting them as the many sons of God (John 3:5-6; Heb. 2:10).

2. As the Spirit of the Son

The Spirit is the Spirit of the Son to cry "Abba, Father" in the believers' heart and to lead the believers to walk as the sons of God (Gal. 4:6; Rom. 8:14-16). Whenever we say "Abba, Father," we touch the Spirit. Galatians 4 says it is the Spirit within us who cries "Abba, Father," whereas Romans 8 says it is we who cry "Abba, Father" in our spirit. This means that the Spirit and our spirit do the same thing. When we cry "Abba, Father" in our spirit from our heart, that is the Spirit's crying.

3. As the Spirit for the Priesthood
of the Gospel to Sanctify the Believers

The Spirit is for the priesthood of the gospel to sanctify

the believers (Rom. 15:16). Whenever we preach the gospel, we fulfill our priesthood of the gospel, and when we fulfill our priesthood, the Spirit goes along with us to sanctify the new believers.

4. To Intercede for the Believers

According to Romans 8:26, the Spirit intercedes for the believers. This is another aspect of the Spirit as the blessing of the gospel.

5. To Renew the Believers

The Spirit also functions to renew the believers, making them the new creation of God (Titus 3:5b; 2 Cor. 5:17). Thus, we have seen the Spirit's regenerating, crying and leading, sanctifying, interceding, and renewing to make us not only the sons of God but also the new creation. Such a wonderful Spirit is the blessing of the gospel.

The Spirit is the reality of the new testament. The unique bequest of the new testament is the Spirit as the consummated Triune God. He is within us. He is sealing us, saturating us, transforming us, and causing us to walk as the sons of God to make us a new creation.

Thurs Review

3. The Holy Spirit anoints seals the believers. To seal is to anoint. The Spirit is a living seal that saturates us w/ the divine element. This sealing Spirit b/co a pledge to the believers that guarantees that God is our inheritance & gives us a fortaste of our inheritance. We need the sealing for us to be God's inheritance. For us to have God as our inheritance we need the pledging.

1.

Fri. trainees speaking

1. The 5 ingredients of the holy anointing: 4 spices + olive oil. 1) Myrrh X death 2) fragrant cinnamon - sweetness & effectiveness of X death 3) calamus the resurrection of X 4) cassia. power of X resurrection. Compounded w/ olive oil which signifies the Spirit & 6: Myrrh 500 sheckles, + 500 shekels of calamus, 250 of cinnamon + 250 of calamus. - This signifies God mingling w/ man to make his His tabernacle

CHAPTER FIVE

THE DEFINITION OF THE SPIRIT

(4)

Scripture Reading: Rev. 1:4-5a; 4:5; 5:6; 2:7, 11, 17, 29; 3:6, 13, 22; Rom. 8:2; John 20:22; Acts 1:8; 2:2, 4, 17; Rev. 22:17a; 21:1—22:5

OUTLINE

II. In the New Testament the Spirit is:
  E. The seven Spirits—Rev. 1:4-5a; 4:5; 5:6:
    1. The sevenfold intensified Spirit for the church's degradation in the dark age.
    2. Ranked as the second in the Divine Trinity instead of the third, indicating the intensification of the Spirit—1:4-5a.
    3. As the seven lamps burning before the throne of God to carry out the divine administration for the consummation of the divine economy—4:5.
    4. As the seven eyes of the Lamb, the observing parts of our Redeemer, to observe all the churches in all the nations for the building up of His Body to consummate the building up of the New Jerusalem, accomplishing the eternal economy of God—5:6; 21:1-3.
    5. To be the speaking Spirit to all the churches—Rev. 2:7, 11, 17, 29; 3:6, 13, 22.
  F. The essential Spirit and the economical Spirit of the processed Triune God:
    1. The essential Spirit of God, the Spirit of life,

breathed into the believers as the divine essence
of the divine life—Rom. 8:2; John 20:22.

2. The economical Spirit of God, the Spirit of
power, poured out upon the believers as the
divine essence of the divine power—Acts 1:8;
2:2, 4, 17.

G. The consummation of the processed Triune God:

1. The Spirit and the bride speak together as the
universal couple—Rev. 22:17a.

2. The processed and consummated Triune God marries the redeemed, regenerated, and transformed
tripartite people for His final manifestation and
ultimate expression in glory for eternity—Rev.
21:1—22:5.

We have seen that in the Old Testament, the Spirit is revealed simply as the Spirit of God, the Spirit of Jehovah, and the Spirit of holiness. But when we come to the New Testament, the revelation concerning the Spirit is very complicated. According to the New Testament revelation, the Spirit has passed through a number of stages. Of course, He was the Spirit of God, the Spirit of Jehovah, and the Spirit of holiness throughout the Old Testament. Throughout these four thousand years of human history, the Spirit of God never changed. But to say that God the Spirit has never changed is a big mistake. This is because after four thousand years of human history, the Triune God Himself entered into a period of time in which He passed through many processes. These processes were incarnation, human living, crucifixion, resurrection, and ascension. Now He is working in His heavenly ministry, which will be concluded at His second coming.

Hebrews 1 says that He will come the second time, not as the only begotten Son of God but as the Firstborn (vv. 5-6). As the only begotten Son of God, He possesses merely divinity. But He will come the second time not mainly in His divine status but in His human status. Before His incarnation Christ, the divine One, already was the only begotten Son of God (John 1:18; Rom. 8:3). By incarnation He put on an element, the human flesh, which had nothing to do with divinity. Then He went through death and entered into resurrection. In resurrection His humanity was "sonized," was made divine. Resurrection was a birth to Christ (Acts 13:33), and in that birth Christ in His humanity was born to be the firstborn Son of God (Rom. 8:29; 1:4). In resurrection He brought His humanity into the divine sonship. Now as the firstborn Son of God, He possesses humanity as well as divinity.

Furthermore, as the Firstborn He brought forth many sons in the same birth and on the same day. On the day of His resurrection, not only He but also all God's chosen people were begotten (1 Pet. 1:3). Since He was the Firstborn, surely there were many others to follow Him. Millions of others were born with Him on the same day, the day of resurrection. He was the Firstborn; and we are the many-born sons of God.

In His resurrection He was also made the life-giving Spirit (1 Cor. 15:45b). That was the consummation of God's processes. Since the Triune God has gone through so many processes, how could the Spirit of God have remained the same, without any change? Actually, the Spirit of God has undergone a great change. The Spirit changed into the Holy Spirit for the bringing forth of Christ into humanity, for His conception (Matt. 1:18, 20). At that point the Spirit of God entered into a new age with a new title—*the Holy Spirit*. Actually, the literal translation of *the Holy Spirit* is "the Spirit the Holy." This means the Spirit is the Holy One. Only God is "the Holy." In the New Testament age, the first thing God did was to enter into man for the purpose of making man God, not in the Godhead, but in life and nature. He became God in man that man might become God so that man might be holy. Now not only God is holy; the man made by God can also be holy (Eph. 1:4; 1 Pet. 1:15-16).

At the beginning of the New Testament, we see the Holy Spirit, but He was still not yet "the Spirit." This is unveiled in John 7:39, which says, "The Spirit was not yet." The Spirit was not yet because Jesus in His humanity had not yet been glorified. Because Jesus in His humanity had not yet been changed, the Holy Spirit who brought forth Jesus through His conception and birth still remained the same, without change. It was not until Jesus was resurrected into His glory, that "the Spirit" who shall flow out of the believers as rivers of living water began to exist. This truth is a big "missing" among Christians today. Andrew Murray said that when "the Spirit" came into existence, this was a "new era," a new age. He had the boldness to say that humanity had been constituted into the Spirit. From the time of Christ's resurrection, whatever has been constituted and wrought into Christ has been consummated in the Spirit. Today the Spirit of God is "the Spirit" who flows out of the believers in Christ as rivers of living water.

First Corinthians 15:45b says, "The last Adam became a life-giving Spirit." This is another "missing" among today's

Christians. The last Adam was Jesus in the flesh. He lived in the flesh for thirty-three and a half years. Then through resurrection, He changed by becoming a life-giving Spirit. This word *became* in Greek is the same word used in John 1:14: "The Word *became* flesh." Thus, the Spirit changed from the Spirit of God to the Spirit who gives life, the life-giving Spirit. First Corinthians 15:45 is a great verse in the Bible. Today some in Christianity pay much attention to John 1:14, but they do not see that the last Adam, who was flesh, became something further. In the first step, He was the Word becoming flesh. In the second step, He was the flesh becoming the life-giving Spirit. We have to see this.

The third "missing" among today's Christians is that they do not see that the life-giving Spirit is the consummation of the Triune God. At the completion of Christ's resurrection, He revealed this divine title to His disciples: *the Father, the Son, and the Holy Spirit* (Matt. 28:19). He passed through incarnation, human living, and death and entered into resurrection. In resurrection the Triune God was consummated by Jesus becoming the life-giving Spirit. Thus, it was not until the resurrection was completed, that this title—the Father, the Son, and the Holy Spirit—was clearly revealed in full. The consummation of the Divine Trinity is the consummated Spirit.

[handwritten margin note: By Jesus becoming the life-giving Spirit we can be baptised in; brought into the complete 3-1 God.]

Also, in the Bible there is a clear vision that the life-giving Spirit has been compounded. He is the compounded Spirit, and within Him there is not only the divine element but also the human element. This is why I treasure chapter five of Andrew Murray's book *The Spirit of Christ*. Andrew Murray had the boldness to stress repeatedly that humanity is now an ingredient of the Spirit. The compound ointment in Exodus 30 is a marvelous type of the compound anointing Spirit. According to this type, the death of Christ with its effectiveness and the resurrection of Christ with its power are ingredients of the compound Spirit. The Spirit today is an ointment. A single item cannot be an ointment. An ointment is a compound of a number of elements. This is the fourth "missing" today.

The fifth "missing" is the seven Spirits spoken of in the book of Revelation (1:4; 4:5; 5:6). To study the definition of the Spirit, we have to get into and stress these five "missings," which are covered in these messages. The life-giving Spirit is the compound Spirit, and this compound Spirit is the seven Spirits.

E. The Seven Spirits

1. The Sevenfold Intensified Spirit

The book of Revelation reveals the seven Spirits as the sevenfold intensified Spirit for the church's degradation in the dark age. Even by the end of the first century, the church had become degraded. The apostles Paul, Peter, and John all dealt with this degradation in their writings—particularly in 2 Timothy, 2 Peter, and the three Epistles of John. At the end of the first century, the degradation of the church began and has continued until today.

Throughout the past nineteen centuries, God has been carrying out His economy; on the other hand, Satan has been carrying out his chaos. We published a book on this subject entitled *The Satanic Chaos in the Old Creation and the Divine Economy for the New Creation*. The satanic chaos and the divine economy go together. Eventually, the satanic chaos will be done away with in the lake of fire, and the divine economy will consummate in the New Jerusalem. In the universe there are both day and night. When you see the church in the day, in a wonderful state, you should be ready to take the night. But when you are in the night, do not be disappointed. Soon the day will come. Because of the degradation in the dark age, God has intensified His Spirit sevenfold.

When the Lord was on this earth for thirty-three and a half years, He did everything by the Spirit, but the Spirit was still just one. With the early apostles at the time of Pentecost, the Spirit was also one. But in the age of Revelation, the Spirit has been intensified sevenfold. Such an intensified Spirit is for us to be vitalized, to be the overcomers in the degradation of the church. At the end of the first century, it was not easy to overcome. Today with us it is the same. In this dark age we need the sevenfold intensified Spirit. Many Christians appreciate what is recorded in the four Gospels and the Acts at Peter's time, but they should appreciate even more what we have today. Today what we experience is the sevenfold intensified Spirit. In order to be the overcomers, we need such a Spirit.

The book of Revelation is a book concerning the overcomers, and the overcomers are the martyrs. In Revelation 12 the man-child is a composition of all the overcoming martyrs beginning from Abel (v. 5). Then all the overcomers standing on the glassy sea in Revelation 15 were martyred by Antichrist during the three and a half years of the great tribulation (v. 2). The overcomers recorded in Revelation are martyrs to God. They lived as martyrs by the sevenfold Spirit.

During the Boxer Rebellion in China, there were a number of Christians who were martyred for the Lord. One brother who was a young businessman in the old capital of Peking told me a story of one young person who was martyred there. One day the Boxers were parading and shouting in the street. All the stores had closed their doors, and he was within his store observing them through a crack in the door. He saw a young girl in their midst singing and praising while being led to her execution by the Boxers. He was amazed that such a young girl would not be afraid in such a terrifying situation. He resolved to find out what made this young woman so courageous. Because of this, he was saved by the Lord and became a preacher. Later he came to my hometown and told me this story. How could such a young girl be that strong? She could be that strong only by the sevenfold intensified Spirit. In order to be today's overcoming martyrs, we need to experience this Spirit.

2. Ranked as the Second in the Divine Trinity

In Revelation 1 the sevenfold Spirit is ranked as the second in the Divine Trinity instead of the third, indicating the intensification of the Spirit (vv. 4-5a).

3. As the Seven Lamps Burning
before the Throne of God

Revelation 4:5 says that the seven Spirits are the seven

lamps burning before the throne of God to carry out the divine
administration for the consummation of the divine economy.
God's administration today is not weak. The administration
of God today on this earth to accomplish His economy is
strong in a sevenfold way. The sevenfold Spirit is the seven
lamps of fire before the throne of God to direct the world situation in order to execute God's economy in the universe.

4. As the Seven Eyes of the Lamb

The seven Spirits are the seven eyes of the Lamb, the
observing parts of our Redeemer, to observe all the churches
in all the nations for the building up of His Body to consummate the building up of the New Jerusalem, accomplishing the
eternal economy of God (Rev. 5:6; 21:1-3). Eventually, the
life-giving Spirit, the compound Spirit, has become the sevenfold Spirit as the seven eyes of the Lamb. This exposes the
wrong teaching that Christ and the Spirit are separate. The
seven Spirits are the eyes of Christ. How could your eyes be
separate from you? They are a part of you. A person's eyes are
for observing and transfusing. When you look at someone, you
observe him and your looking at him transfuses something of
you into him. The sevenfold Spirit today is the eyes of our
Savior. He observes us and transfuses all His riches into us by
His seven eyes.

5. To Be the Speaking Spirit to All the Churches

The sevenfold intensified Spirit is the speaking Spirit to
all the churches. The Lord's epistles to the seven churches are
in Revelation 2 and 3. At the beginning of each epistle, it was
the Lord Jesus speaking (2:1, 8, 12, 18; 3:1, 7, 14), yet at the
end of each epistle it says that whoever has an ear should
listen to what the Spirit says to all the churches (2:7, 11, 17,
29; 3:6, 13, 22).

He is the speaking Spirit in the beginning of the book of
Revelation. Then He becomes the consummated Spirit as
the totality of the Triune God at the end of Revelation. Today
He speaks to the churches, but at the end He and the
church speak together, and the church is His bride (Rev.
22:17a). The processed Triune God consummated as the Spirit

is married to the redeemed, regenerated, transformed, glorified tripartite man as His wife. The Triune God and the tripartite man become a married couple. The New Jerusalem as the conclusion of the Bible is the marriage life of the processed God married to the transformed man. They live together as a couple in eternity, and their life is portrayed in full in the New Jerusalem.

F. The Essential Spirit and the Economical Spirit of the Processed Triune God

The essential Spirit of God is the Spirit of life breathed into the believers as the divine essence of the divine life (Rom. 8:2; John 20:22). The economical Spirit of God, the Spirit of power, was poured out upon the believers as the divine essence of the divine power (Acts 1:8; 2:2, 4, 17). The consummated Spirit has these two aspects: the inward, essential aspect and the outward, economical aspect. On the day of resurrection, the Lord breathed the essential Spirit as life into His disciples. Then after fifty days, on the day of Pentecost, He poured out the economical Spirit of power upon the disciples. The essential Spirit is for our life and living inwardly. The economical Spirit is for our ministry and work outwardly. To be economical means to be for God's economy, for God's work, to carry out His plan.

The Lord Jesus also experienced the Spirit in these two aspects. He was born of the Spirit, filled up with the Spirit, and constituted with the Spirit. But when He became thirty years of age to come out to do the work for God to carry out God's economy, the Holy Spirit came upon Him in the form of a dove (Matt. 3:16). This was the economical aspect of the Spirit for Christ to carry out God's economy.

G. The Consummation of the Processed Triune God

1. The Spirit and the Bride Speaking Together as the Universal Couple

Ultimately, the Spirit is the consummation of the processed Triune God. This is the consummation of the Triune

God after His ascension, that is, after He had been fully processed. Such a Spirit speaks together with the bride as the
universal couple (Rev. 22:17a).

2. The Processed and Consummated Triune God Married to His Redeemed, Regenerated, and Transformed Tripartite People

The conclusion of the entire sixty-six books of the Bible
reveals that the processed and consummated Triune God
marries the redeemed, regenerated, and transformed tripartite
people for His final manifestation and ultimate expression in
glory for eternity (Rev. 21:1—22:5). We may wonder what the
difference is between *manifestation* and *expression*. Something that is concealed can be manifested, uncovered, or
disclosed. God was concealed as a mystery. But when Jesus
came, He was God's manifestation. Then this manifestation
has an issue, and the issue is to express God. The Triune God
will have the New Jerusalem as His corporate manifestation.
Then through that manifestation He will be expressed corpo-
rately for eternity.

CHAPTER SIX

THE DEFINITION OF OUR SPIRIT

Scripture Reading: 1 Thes. 5:23; Heb. 4:12b; Gen. 2:7; Zech. 12:1b; Isa. 42:5; Luke 9:23-25; Job 32:8; Prov. 20:27; John 4:24; 2 Tim. 4:22a; Gen. 2:9b; 1:27; 1 Cor. 6:17; Rom. 9:1; 8:16; 1:9; Luke 1:47; 1 Cor. 2:11; Mark 2:8

OUTLINE

I. We being created by God a tripartite being—1 Thes. 5:23; Heb. 4:12b:
   A. With a body formed of the dust, as our outward frame—Gen. 2:7a.
   B. With a spirit produced of God's breath, as our intrinsic organ, ranked with the heavens and the earth—Gen. 2:7b; Zech. 12:1b; Isa. 42:5.
   C. With a soul, the issue of our spirit being added to our body, as our self in between our body and our spirit—Gen. 2:7c; Luke 9:23-25.
II. Our spirit being particularly created by God as our particular organ—Gen. 2:7b:
   A. With the breath of God—Job 32:8.
   B. As the lamp of Jehovah—Prov. 20:27.
   C. For us to worship God—to contact and contain God—John 4:24; 2 Tim. 4:22a.
   D. For us to receive God as life and to express God—Gen. 2:9b; 1:27.
   E. For us to be joined to God as one spirit—1 Cor. 6:17.
III. The composition of our spirit:
   A. The conscience—Rom. 9:1; cf. Rom. 8:16.
   B. The fellowship—John 4:24; Rom. 1:9; Luke 1:47.
   C. The intuition—1 Cor. 2:11; Mark 2:8.

In the previous messages, we have seen the definition of the Spirit. In order to help us see the truth concerning the Spirit in a full way, I would encourage us to read and even to study a small booklet we have published entitled *The Spirit of the Glorified Jesus*. This booklet is a reprint of chapter five of Andrew Murray's book *The Spirit of Christ*. Andrew Murray points out that today's Spirit has not only the divine element but also the human element. This is an extraordinary revelation. In the Spirit there are also the elements of Christ's death and resurrection.

Today the Spirit is not only the Spirit of divinity but also the Spirit of Christ's humanity. In 1971 we gave a number of messages on the significance of the meal offering in the book of Leviticus. In those messages we stressed that the meal offering refers to Christ's humanity (see the book entitled *Christ as the Reality*). In those messages we coined a new term by saying that we should be "Jesusly human."

In resurrection Christ, who was the only begotten Son of God in His divinity, was born of God in His humanity to be the firstborn Son of God (Acts 13:33; Rom. 8:29; 1:4). His humanity was "sonized," made divine. This "sonizing" in resurrection sanctified, uplifted, and transformed Christ's humanity which He put on in incarnation. Today such an uplifted humanity is in the Spirit and can be our enjoyment in the Spirit.

I hope that we could spend some time to study the previous messages we have released concerning the Spirit. If our understanding and apprehension of the Spirit are limited, we will not enjoy the Spirit as much as we should. Our learning and our study of the divine revelation will help us to participate in, to enjoy, the all-inclusive compounded Spirit, in whom we have Christ's divinity, Christ's humanity, Christ's death, and Christ's resurrection. Andrew Murray said that the humanity of Jesus has been interwoven into His divinity. He used the word *interwoven,* as in a textile. We use the word *mingled,* as in the mingling of the fine flour with oil in the meal offering (Lev. 2:4).

Our study of the Spirit of God in the previous outlines and messages was simple, but I believe it was all-inclusive. Those outlines and messages are the produce, the abstract, and the crystallization of the proper understanding of the Spirit of God according to the holy Word. Without such a Spirit, the humanity of Christ uplifted through resurrection could not be ours. Today the Spirit is the instrument which conveys all the elements of Christ's person and Christ's work into our being. Christ's divinity, His humanity, His death with its effectiveness, and His resurrection with its power remain in us. But due to our lack of the proper understanding, we do not know how to enjoy them. This is like having groceries without knowing how to cook them so that we can eat them. We need to see that today all the elements of Christ's person and work can be our enjoyment in the Spirit.

Now that we have seen the definition of the Spirit, we want to see the definition of our human spirit. This definition is very simple, but we should not minimize it. It is very simple yet very vital and crucial in the divine and spiritual realm. God is a Spirit. This is strongly and emphatically taught by the Bible. The Bible also strongly stresses and teaches us concerning the human spirit. This is a big "missing" in today's Christianity. They miss the human spirit even more than they miss the proper understanding of the Spirit of God.

When I began to minister in the United States in 1962, a number of people told me that they had never before heard that man has a spirit. Many teachers and preachers do not know or believe the truth concerning the human spirit. In 1954 I was invited to hold a conference and training in Hong Kong. A certain Brethren missionary came to Hong Kong to attend my conference. After the conference he told me that he appreciated what he heard in the meetings but that he could not agree with the teaching about the human spirit. He said that the *spirit* and the *soul* are synonyms, referring to the same thing. I asked him about 1 Thessalonians 5:23, where Paul refers to our "spirit and soul and body." Paul used the conjunction *and* twice in this phrase. This shows that man's spirit and soul are two distinct items. Furthermore, Hebrews 4:12 says that the living word of God can divide our spirit from our soul. After I pointed this out to him, he still said that he could not believe that we have a human spirit. Many dear saints today are like this. Some do not care about the spirit and the soul. They feel that this is too abstract to talk about. It is no wonder that they cannot be spiritual. Actually, you can never be spiritual if you do not know you have a spirit.

John 4:24 says that God is Spirit. This means that God's substance is Spirit. This verse goes on to say that those who worship Him must worship Him in spirit—the human spirit. The divine Spirit and the human spirit are both mentioned in John 4:24. The Gospel of John has another verse which refers to the two spirits. John 3:6 says, "That which is born of the Spirit is spirit." In this verse the first Spirit is the begetting Spirit; the second spirit is the begotten spirit. Romans 8:16 says that the Spirit witnesses with our spirit. The pronoun *our* is used in this verse, referring to our human spirit. God is Spirit, but if we had no spirit, we could not join to Him as one spirit. This is mentioned emphatically in 1 Corinthians 6:17: "He who is joined to the Lord is one spirit." These are the strong verses in the New Testament which convey the revelation to us concerning both God the Spirit and our spirit.

If God were not a Spirit, how could He be our life? If we did not have a spirit, how could God be contacted, touched, received, and contained by us? This would be impossible. Our spirit is the organ with which we can contact God the Spirit. We must use the proper organ to contact God. In order to see, we must use our eyes. We cannot appreciate colors if we do not use our eyes, the proper organ. People say there is no God, because they are unaware that they have a particular organ within them with which to contact God. They deny this organ and do not use it, so they cannot know God. God is a Spirit, and He made a spirit within us so that we can contact Him.

I. WE BEING CREATED BY GOD A TRIPARTITE BEING

In the record of God's creation in Genesis, God did not give us many details concerning the heavens because the heavens do not have that much direct relationship with us. But concerning the earth, God gave us a number of details. Genesis

1:2 through Genesis 2 gives us the details of the earth. First, God caused the dry land to appear on the third day. Then He made the plant life and the animal life. Eventually, God told us that He made man.

In God's creation, He mostly spoke things into being, but in His creation of man, He used two substances. Genesis 2:7 says that He used the dust to make man's body and His breath of life to form man's spirit. The breath of life is not God Himself, God's life, or God's Spirit. But it is very close to God, very close to the life of God, and very close to the Spirit of God.

Before the breath of life entered into man, he just had a lifeless frame. But when the breath of life entered into man's frame, man became a living soul. The soul was not created by God out of a certain substance. The soul was the issue of the breath of life entering into man's body. It is man's being, man's self. Exodus tells us that seventy souls of the house of Jacob went down to Egypt (1:5). These were seventy persons. A person is a soul. This shows us that the soul is our very person, our being. The soul is between the outward frame, the body, and the inward organ, the spirit.

A. With a Body Formed of the Dust, as Our Outward Frame

In studying the definition of our spirit, we must be clear about God's creation. We have been created by God as a tripartite man. As we have seen, 1 Thessalonians 5:23 and Hebrews 4:12b are the most basic verses in the Bible concerning man's three parts. Man's body formed of the dust is his outward frame (Gen. 2:7a). The minerals in our body are the minerals of the dust.

B. With a Spirit Produced of God's Breath, as Our Intrinsic Organ, Ranked with the Heavens and the Earth

We also have a spirit produced of God's breath, as our intrinsic organ, ranked with the heavens and the earth (Gen. 2:7b; Zech. 12:1b; Isa. 42:5). I do not use the word *made* or *created* but *produced*. The breath of life *produced* the spirit.

Actually, it was the breath of life becoming the spirit. In Genesis 2:7 the Hebrew word for "breath," *neshamah,* is the same word used for "spirit" in Proverbs 20:27, which speaks of the spirit of man.

We have two main organs. One is the body as our outward organ, which is full of functions. But we also have an intrinsic organ within us—our spirit. We can substantiate all the things in the divine, spiritual, and heavenly field by our spirit. If we do not use our spirit, we become very low, like the beasts. The difference between man and the other living creatures is that only man has a spirit (Job 12:10). The spirit distinguishes us from all the animals, so we must study our spirit and exercise our spirit. If we do not care for our spirit, we can never enjoy God, we can never be spiritual, and we can never grow in the divine life.

C. With a Soul, the Issue of
Our Spirit Being Added to Our Body

The soul is not a substance. It is an issue of two substances coming together. When the breath of God came into the body of dust, an issue came out. This issue is our soul as our self in between our body and our spirit (Gen. 2:7c; Luke 9:23-25). The more that we experience the spiritual life and enjoy God, the more we realize this matter of our soul being between our body and our spirit. Whether we are for the body or for the spirit depends upon what we let our soul do.

Let us suppose you have a choice between two things. One thing would cause you to lose your temper, but the other thing would cause you to praise God. Which thing would you welcome? This is up to the decision of your soul. In the evening you may have the choice between two things. You can either go to the church meeting or stay home and watch television. Which would you choose? At that juncture it is very clear that going to the meeting is the spirit's intention, whereas staying home to watch television is the fleshly desire of your fallen body. This shows that the soul is between our body and our spirit.

Day by day we are confronted with things and situations

in which we must decide whether to follow our fallen body or our regenerated spirit. Sometimes we may have a choice between making a telephone call or making a "call to the heavens" to pray. We may be addicted to gossiping with someone who is our friend. This kind of talk is in our soul with our body. The desire to make a call to the heavens, to talk to the Lord, is of the Spirit and in the spirit. Quite often, however, we may choose to make phone calls instead of calling to the heavens. When we make vain phone calls, our spirit will be deadened. When we do this, we should confess, "Lord, forgive me. Today I disobeyed You in making many calls that were not according to You. Lord, I realize that those telephone calls were of the flesh and selected by my soul." These illustrations show that the soul is between the spirit and the body.

II. OUR SPIRIT BEING PARTICULARLY CREATED BY GOD AS OUR PARTICULAR ORGAN

Genesis 2:7, a short verse of the Bible, gives us three points. First, God made man with the dust. Second, God breathed into man's nostrils the breath of life. Third, a living soul, a human being, came out as an issue. The making of the body and the issue of the soul were not as important as the producing of the spirit. The most crucial thing was the producing of the spirit. If we had only a soul with a body, we would be like the beasts.

Most people live by the soul with the body. The newspapers always give reports of people who are involved in evil things such as robbery, stealing, fornication, divorce, and murder. These are people who are living by their soul with their body. We need to be different. We should endeavor to live by our spirit with the Spirit. We should deny our ugly, contaminated soul and reject our dirty, fallen body.

The Bible tells us to deny the soul because it has been corrupted (Matt. 16:24-26; Luke 9:23-25). One day when Peter was talking to the Lord, Satan came out of him, even through his loving of the Lord (Matt. 16:22-23). The soul is ugly, and we should hate it. The body is dirty, and we should reject it. We Christians who are under God's teaching should always endeavor to live by our spirit with the Spirit. It is in our spirit that we have the real rest. We are different than most people. While they live by their soul with their body, we live by our spirit with the Spirit.

A. With the Breath of God

Job 32:8 says, "But there is a spirit in man, / And the breath of the Almighty gives them understanding." According to the poetic structure of this verse, the spirit and the breath of God, the Almighty, are in apposition. Thus, the spirit is the breath of God, and the breath of God is the spirit. Job 32:8 shows that God made our spirit with the breath of God.

B. As the Lamp of Jehovah

Proverbs 20:27 says that the spirit of man is the lamp of Jehovah. When God created man, He put a lamp into man. Among all the creatures, only man has an inner lamp. God created a spirit within man as God's lamp, but this lamp does not function. This is why most of the human race is in darkness, without light. One day, however, we were saved by repenting and believing into the Lord Jesus. When we did this, we began to feel that something within us was shining to enlighten us. That was the functioning of our spirit as the lamp of the Lord.

In ancient times a lamp burned to give forth its light by the oil within it. The oil typifies the Spirit of God (Isa. 61:1). We have our spirit as a lamp and we always have to contact God through this lamp. Then this lamp will be refilled all the time (Eph. 5:18). The light shining in the lamp comes from the oil, the Spirit. Furthermore, when the oil burns in the lamp to shine, the oil has mingled itself with the lamp. When the oil soaks the wick, the oil and the wick become one. Then they burn together. On the one hand, the wick is burning; on the other hand, the oil is burning. Without the wick, the oil could not burn, and without the oil, the wick could not burn. They must be mingled together by soaking. This shows that we can be soaked by God and with God in our spirit, which is the lamp of God.

C. For Us to Worship God

Our spirit was created by God as our particular organ for us to worship God—to contact and contain God (John 4:24; 2 Tim. 4:22a). We cannot worship God without contacting Him. To worship God actually is to contact God. John 4:24 says that those who worship God must worship Him in spirit. Then 2 Timothy 4:22a says that the Lord Jesus is with our spirit. How could someone be with our spirit? I can be with you, but I cannot be with you in your spirit. Only the Lord Jesus can be with us in our spirit, because He is the life-giving Spirit (1 Cor. 15:45b). Our spirit is a container and a recipient of the Lord. Thank the Lord that we have a spirit. First, God created our spirit; second, He regenerated our spirit; third, He strengthens our spirit; and fourth, He refills our spirit.

D. For Us to Receive God as Life and to Express God

Such a spirit is for us to receive God as life and to express Him (Gen. 2:9b; 1:27). We are living on this earth for the purpose of receiving God and expressing God.

E. For Us to Be Joined to God as One Spirit

Eventually, we can be joined to God as one spirit (1 Cor. 6:17). In the whole universe, nothing can be higher than to be joined to God as one spirit. The divine Spirit and the human spirit become one spirit. If all human beings were joined together with God as one spirit, the earth would become heaven! The earth is full of bad news because people live by their soul with their body. But we need to be those who live by our spirit with the Spirit.

III. THE COMPOSITION OF OUR SPIRIT

Our spirit is composed of the conscience, the fellowship, and the intuition. For a further discussion of the functions of our spirit, see pages 56-59 of *The Economy of God.*

A. The Conscience

In Romans 9:1 Paul said that his conscience bore witness

with him in the Holy Spirit. Romans 8:16 says that the Spirit witnesses with our spirit. On the one hand, the Holy Spirit bears witness with our spirit. On the other hand, our conscience bears witness with the Holy Spirit. This shows that the conscience is a function of our spirit. If we neglect our conscience, our spirit cannot function properly to contact the Spirit. We must learn to take care of our conscience. The conscience regulates us by either condemning or justifying us. Our inner justification and inner condemnation is by our conscience in our spirit.

B. The Fellowship

The fellowship is another function of our spirit. John 4:24 says God is Spirit and those who worship Him must worship Him in spirit. To worship Him means to fellowship with Him. If you are going to fellowship with God, you must do it in your spirit. Outside of the spirit, there is no fellowship with God. In Romans 1:9 Paul said that he served God in his spirit. To serve God is to fellowship with God. The servants and the master always contact each other. They always fellowship. We serve God, our Master, by contacting Him, fellowshipping with Him, in our spirit. Luke 1:47 says, "My spirit has exulted in God my Savior." To exult in God, to be joyful in the Lord, is also a kind of fellowship.

C. The Intuition

First Corinthians 2:11 says that only the spirit of man knows the things of man. This is a direct knowledge from the intuition. Mark 2:8 tells us that even the Lord Jesus, while He was on this earth, perceived in His spirit. He had the Holy Spirit with Him, but He also was a man with His own spirit. He had the inward intuition in His spirit to directly perceive things.

God created man in a particular way, w/ a human spirit. This was made w/ the highest material in the universe—God's breath. God's econ is carried out in our spirit. It is a blessing to be brought here to see our spirit—this ministry is a blessing & a gift. The enemy veils man concerning our spirit. We are trained to see normal believers in Christ. A normal Xian knows & exercises our spirit. To be a spiritual man is one whose spirit takes the lead in every thing we do. We are learning how to do this day by day. This is a life long learning. The human spirit is ranked among the heavens & the earth. Do we have a vision that we have a human spirit. We have to worship God in our spirit. The soul is a vessel made to contain God. It is a great release to see God's arrangement for our lives in their entirety. It is a great release to see God's arrangement & sovereignty. The soul should be under God's arrangement, under the direction of the Spirit in our spirit.

CHAPTER SEVEN

THE IMPORTANCE
OF OUR HUMAN SPIRIT

Scripture Reading: Zech. 12:1b; Prov. 20:27; Job 32:8; John
4:24; 2 Tim. 4:22a; Rom. 8:11; Eph. 2:22; Rom. 8:4b; 12:11;
1 Cor. 2:11a, 15a; Acts 17:16; 19:21; 20:22; Rom. 1:9; Rev. 1:10;
4:2; 17:3; 21:10; Acts 18:25

OUTLINE

I. In the eyes of God—ranked with the heavens and the
earth—Zech. 12:1b.

II. In our worshiping of God—John 4:24.

III. In Christ and the Spirit indwelling us, <u>taking our
spirit as God's habitation</u>—2 Tim. 4:22a; Rom. 8:11;
Eph. 2:22. *Christ is the embodiment of G. He is the life-giving Spirit in our spirit. The entire 3-1 G. is in our spirit.*

IV. In our Christian walk—Rom. 8:4b.

V. In our service to the Lord—Rom. 12:11 *w/o our spirit we cannot serve God.*

VI. Except the spirit of man, no man knows the things of
man, <u>but the spiritual man discerns all things</u>—1 Cor.
2:11a, 15a.

VII. The apostles lived in their spirit:
A. Paul—Acts 17:16; 19:21; 20:22; Rom. 1:9.
B. John—Rev. 1:10; 4:2; 17:3; 21:10. *← everything he saw in Rev was when he was in spirit.*
C. Apollos—Acts 18:25.

Then we become a spiritual man.

We need to be impressed with the proper knowledge of our human spirit. We have seen that in God's creation, God paid the most attention to the creation of our spirit. Genesis 1:1 tells us that God created the heavens and the earth. Then verse 2 shows how the universe was damaged because of Satan's rebellion, telling us that the earth became waste and void, and darkness was upon the face of the deep. Genesis 1 goes on to show how God recovered the damaged universe. He recovered the earth by bringing in the light, and He caused the dry land to appear on the third day. Then He created all kinds of plant life and animal life. When God was creating man, the environment for man's existence had been fully prepared.

In God's creation, He also prepared a garden for man. God brought man into that garden, indicating that this garden would be man's residence. The garden of Eden was full of trees which were pleasant to the sight and good for food. Man was placed in the midst of this garden before the tree of life, alongside of which was another tree, the tree of the knowledge of good and evil (Gen. 2:8-9). This garden was a complete scene of the entire earth. The tree of life signifies God, and the tree of the knowledge of good and evil signifies the evil one, Satan.

God brought Adam into that garden and charged him to be careful about his eating. He indicated that all the trees were good for food, including the tree of life. But there was one tree of which Adam was not to eat, the tree of the knowledge of good and evil (vv. 16-17). Knowledge, good, and evil are three negative things. Life is the unique positive thing. Eventually, knowledge, good, and evil issue in death. The tree of life will lead you out of death, but the tree of knowledge, good, and evil results in death.

God created man in a marvelous way so that man could contact God, contain God, and receive God as life to express God. Genesis not only tells us that God created man in His image and after His likeness but it also tells us how He created man. First, He created a frame for man with the dust from the earth. Then He breathed into this human frame His breath of life (2:7). God's breath of life is the highest material that He can use to create anything. What else is as precious as the breath of God, the breath of life? And that breath of life from God was breathed into the human frame. What a wonderful thing!

After the breath of life entered into man's frame, it became a part of his human constitution. We were constituted firstly with the dust outwardly and secondly with the breath of God inwardly. The outward frame is man's body, and the inward breath of life has become man's spirit. Man's body and man's spirit came together to produce a living soul (Gen. 2:7). The same Hebrew word for "breath" in Genesis 2:7 is translated "spirit," the spirit of man, in Proverbs 20:27. In Job 32:8 man's spirit is in apposition to the breath of God. A human being is a soul with two organs. The outward organ is the body; the inward organ is our spirit, which is the breath of life. Thus, in 1 Thessalonians 5:23 we are told that a whole man is composed of spirit, soul, and body.

Now in the whole universe there are two big categories of things. The first category of things is material, physical. The second category of things in the universe is spiritual. To contact anything physical, you have to use your body, your outward organ. To contact God as the Spirit with all the spiritual things, you have to use your spirit, your inward organ. In the modern culture of today's world, people mostly care for the physical things and neglect the spiritual things. But the Bible uplifts the spiritual things and depreciates the physical things. The Bible even tells us that we need to put to death the practices of our body (Rom. 8:13) and take care of our spirit. We have to uplift our spirit.

If a human being lives by the body, he is very mean, like a beast. But if a human being lives by the spirit, he is very high, higher than the angels. Many unbelievers live in a very low way by their body. Most of them do not know their spirit, but some know one part of their spirit, that is, their human conscience. Some among them live according to their conscience. This is to live partly by the spirit, so these people are higher. Today we believers are charged to deny ourselves, our soul, and to put to death the practices of our body. Then we live by the spirit, walk by the spirit, and do everything according to the spirit. Romans 8:4 says that we need to walk according to the spirit.

Now we want to see the importance of our spirit. In the whole universe, firstly God is important to us. God has the preeminence. Besides God nothing is as important as our human spirit. For something to be important means that it is indispensable, that you must have it. With all other things besides God and besides our spirit, we have a choice. Whether or not we have them is not vitally important. But we must have God and our human spirit. Firstly, God is the Spirit to us. Then we have a human spirit to contact God the Spirit, to receive Him, and to contain Him. He lives in our spirit to be one with us.

I. IN THE EYES OF GOD—
RANKED WITH THE HEAVENS AND THE EARTH

In the eyes of God, our human spirit is ranked with the heavens and the earth. There are two verses in the Bible concerning this one point—Zechariah 12:1 and Isaiah 42:5. Zechariah 12:1 says clearly that God stretched forth the heavens, laid the foundation of the earth, and formed the spirit of man within him. The heavens are for the earth; the earth is for man; and man has a spirit to contact God. We can contact God only by using our spirit.

II. IN OUR WORSHIPING OF GOD

Our human spirit is important in our contacting God, and our contacting God is our worship to God. We cannot contact God without worshiping Him. God is the object of human worship, and the human worship must be carried out by contacting God. If we worship God, we contact Him. We can contact God by using our spirit. The Lord Jesus told us purposely in John 4:24 that God is Spirit and that we must worship Him in our spirit. We worship Him by exercising our spirit. If we are going to live a meaningful life, we should contact God. He is our source, and our spirit is our spiritual organ for us to contact Him.

We live physically by exercising our body. But to merely live physically is no higher than the living of a beast. If we are going to live a super life, a higher life, we have to do it by exercising our spirit, which came from the origin of God's breath of life. This spiritual organ within us is mainly for us to contact God, to worship Him.

We must be deeply impressed with this basic knowledge of the holy Word. We are being trained to be normal believers in Christ. A normal believer's life implies the service, the worship, he should render to the Triune God, and in all of our service we must contact God in our spirit.

III. IN CHRIST AND THE SPIRIT INDWELLING US, TAKING OUR SPIRIT AS GOD'S HABITATION

Our human spirit is important because it is in this spirit that Christ and the Spirit indwell us, taking our spirit as God's habitation (2 Tim. 4:22a; Rom. 8:11; Eph. 2:22). If you do not have God in your spirit, your soul will also be empty. The soul was made to be a vessel to contain God as the contents. Romans 9 tells us clearly that we human beings are vessels to God, containers to contain God as our contents (vv. 21, 23). Today the Triune God is embodied in Christ and realized as the Spirit. Both the embodiment and the realization of God indwell us, remaining within us to be our contents in our spirit. Because of Their indwelling, we human beings become God's habitation.

The contents of man should be the very creating God, the Triune God. He created us with an organ to receive Him, to take Him in, and to contain Him so that He can come into us to be our contents. If you have a house without a dweller, that is a pitiful house. Our dweller is the Triune God. The New Testament says that God abides in us (1 John 4:16), and it goes on to give us even more details. To merely say that God dwells in us is still too general. God has to be embodied, and God has to be realized. When God is embodied, He becomes Christ (Col. 2:9). When God is realized, He becomes the life-giving Spirit (1 Cor. 15:45b). So today we have Christ and the Spirit dwelling in us, taking us as Their habitation (Eph. 2:22). How wonderful it is to have Christ living in me! How sweet and how pleasant it is to have the life-giving Spirit dwelling in me! We should declare, "Christ lives in me, makes His home in me!" (Eph. 3:17). "The Spirit dwells in me!"

Since Christ and the Spirit indwell us, we become top beings in the whole universe. Our rank is now with God. We become on the level of God and are much higher than the angels. We should be happy because we are the highest beings, ranked with God. We need to realize that we are on the same level with God because we have been born of God (John 1:12-13). If you are born of a cat, you become a cat. One is the originator, and the others are the children. The children are in the rank of the mother. If the mother is a human being, surely all the children are human beings. We are born of the great God, so we become God in His life and nature, but of course, not in His Godhead. We are ranked with God. He is our great Originator, and we are His children. He became a God-man so that man can become a man-God. Eventually, He and we are in the same category, of the same kind, and on the same level.

IV. IN OUR CHRISTIAN WALK

In our Christian walk, we need to walk according to our spirit (Rom. 8:4b). When you ask me a question, I should not answer you from my soul. I should answer you from my spirit. Then I become a spiritual man. Our Christian walk is a spiritual walk. Our soul should be under our spirit's direction with our body under our soul's usage. Then we are spiritual men who walk, live, and have our being according to our spirit.

V. IN OUR SERVICE TO THE LORD

Paul tells us that he served God in his spirit (Rom. 1:9). Then he charged us to be burning in our spirit that we may have the top service rendered to God (Rom. 12:11). Without the exercise of our spirit, we cannot live the Christian life and we cannot serve God.

VI. EXCEPT THE SPIRIT OF MAN, NO MAN KNOWS THE THINGS OF MAN

First Corinthians 2 tells us that the spirit of man knows the things of man (v. 11a) and that the spiritual man discerns all things (v. 15a). Without our spirit, we cannot know who we are. The unbelievers do not know who they are, where they came from, or where they are going. In order to know the things of man, man needs his spirit. Confucius taught that if man is to live the highest life, he must take care of his conscience. If you take care of your conscience, you can realize it is related to Someone in the heavens. Our conscience is a part of our spirit, and our spirit is related to God. Without our spirit we cannot understand the things of man. If we use our spirit to understand the things of man, this will guide us to God. This will lead us to contact God. Our human spirit is the spiritual organ for us to know the things concerning man and eventually to know the things concerning God.

VII. THE APOSTLES LIVED IN THEIR SPIRIT

We can also see the importance of our human spirit in the living of the early apostles. They all lived in their spirit.

A. Paul

The apostle Paul was a person who lived in his spirit (Acts 17:16; 19:21; 20:22; Rom. 1:9).

B. John

John said four times in Revelation that he was in his spirit. He was in his spirit when he saw the vision of the churches (1:10). He was in his spirit when he saw the vision of the destiny of the world (4:2). He was in his spirit when he saw the vision of the great harlot, Babylon the Great, which is degraded Christianity (17:3). Then he told us he was in his spirit to see the New Jerusalem (21:10). To see these four great things, John needed to be in his spirit. We need to be in our spirit to see all the heavenly visions.

C. Apollos

Acts 18:25 says that Apollos was fervent in spirit. He was burning in teaching the Bible. This shows us that all the apostles lived in their spirit. We have to follow their example by living in our spirit—behaving, acting, and walking in our spirit—doing things, thinking things, and speaking things altogether in our spirit. Then eventually, as 1 Corinthians shows, we become a spiritual man (2:15a). Then we can have a proper church life and have the proper and profitable church meetings.

CHAPTER EIGHT

THE EXERCISE OF OUR SPIRIT

Scripture Reading: 2 Tim. 1:6-7; Rom. 8:5-6; Heb. 4:12

OUTLINE

I. To fan our spirit—2 Tim. 1:6-7:
   A. God has not given us a spirit of cowardice, but of power, love, and sobermindedness.
   B. Our spirit is surrounded by the three parts of the soul—will, emotion, and mind:
      1. Our will should be strong, full of power.
      2. Our emotion should be loving, full of love.
      3. Our mind should be sober, full of sobermindedness.
II. To set our mind on the spirit—Rom. 8:5-6:
   A. To set our mind on the flesh is death.
   B. To set our mind on the spirit is life and peace.
III. To discern our spirit from our soul—Heb. 4:12.

It is very good that we can be on the study of our spirit. I can testify that whenever we teach and speak about our human spirit, we have joy. This is because man was created by God with a spirit, and this spirit is a particular organ within man which functions to contact God and contain God. Man was created by God to be a living creature, but he is different from all the other living creatures. Only man has a human spirit.

Genesis tells us clearly that in God's creation, He did something particular to produce our spirit (2:7). God created the universe by speaking. God spoke and it was (Psa. 33:9). But when God came to the creation of man, He breathed His breath of life into man. Our breath is not ourselves, but nothing is as close to us as our breath. In like manner, God's breath of life is not God Himself, not the divine Spirit, and not the divine life, but it is very close to God, close to the divine Spirit, and close to the divine life.

If we did not have a spirit, we would be like the beasts. We would become meaningless. Also, if there were no God in the universe, the whole universe would become empty. So the key to our meaning and the meaning of the universe is in God's existence and also in our having a spirit. God is Spirit and we must contact Him, worship Him, in our spirit (John 4:24). These two spirits should contact each other and should become one (1 Cor. 6:17). Then the whole universe becomes meaningful. Then our life has its meaning. Without God being the Spirit and without us having a spirit to contact God, to be one with God, the whole universe is empty and we are nothing. By this we can see the importance of our spirit.

Regretfully, due to the fall, men have not only overlooked and neglected the human spirit, but also have even refused to admit that man has a spirit. Some men who live a higher life take care of their conscience, but they are in the minority. Most people take care of the law, not their conscience. Today's society needs the law so much because most people neglect one part of their spirit—their conscience. The conscience functions to judge us and condemn us when we do something wrong. Actually, the best people in human society are not the lawful ones, but the ones who take care of their conscience.

Some who are governed merely by the law like to find loopholes in the law so that they can carry out things that are unrighteous and unjust. Those who live by the conscience, however, live in a higher way. Our inward conscience controls us much more than the outward law does.

As Christians, our spirit has been regenerated. To be regenerated is to be reinforced. Something stronger and richer has been added into our being. This is God's life, which has been added into our spirit. This addition is a real gift. Hebrews 6:4 says that we believers have tasted of the heavenly gift. When we believe in the Lord Jesus, God firstly gives us the divine life. Secondly, God gives us the Holy Spirit. Also, He gives us many heavenly things, such as His forgiveness, righteousness, peace, and joy. God has given us justification, reconciliation, and His full salvation. All these were given in addition to God's life and God's Spirit. Actually, all these heavenly things are included in God's life and God's Spirit, which have been added into our spirit. We have a regenerated and reinforced spirit, a very strong spirit, with a companion. This companion is the Triune God. The Triune God becomes our companion in our spirit. What an enriched spirit we have!

Now that we have seen the importance of our spirit, we want to see the exercise of our spirit. We must build up a habit of exercising our spirit. When I rise up in the morning, the first thing I spontaneously say is "O Lord." To call on the Lord by saying, "O Lord" is a habit of exercising our spirit. To say "O Lord" as soon as you rise up in the morning makes a big difference. If you rise up in the morning without saying anything, you may pray in a routine way without really touching the Lord. This is because there is no exercise of your spirit. We have to build up a habit of saying, "O Lord." When we say, "O Lord," we touch the Lord. This is the habit of exercising our spirit.

At times we may be in a hard situation. We may be sick or we may have lost our job. At that time, we should exercise our spirit. We should force ourselves to say, "O Lord Jesus!" The word *exercise* implies forcing. To exercise is always a forced matter. When the Olympic athletes are exercising to practice or compete, they must have a strong will. They force themselves to exercise. If we Christians want to be strong and want to grow in the Lord, we must force ourselves to use our spirit.

Let us suppose that a problem comes into your family life. It may be a problem between you and your spouse, between you and your children, or between you and your parents. If you do not exercise your spirit at that time, your entire soul with your mind, will, and emotion will become prevailing. Then the soul will overcome and subdue you, conquering your spirit. This can even cause you to lose your temper in a bad way. Therefore, whenever you are in a hard situation, you have to force yourself to exercise your spirit. To force yourself to exercise, or to use, your spirit makes you a different person.

In 1 Timothy 4:7 Paul said, "Exercise yourself unto godliness." Then in verse 8 he spoke of bodily exercise. In these two verses Paul speaks of two kinds of exercise. The exercise besides that of the body, which is the exercise unto godliness, must be the exercise of the spirit. To exercise ourselves unto godliness is to exercise our spirit to live Christ in our daily life.

I. TO FAN OUR SPIRIT

Second Timothy 1:6-7 indicates that we need to fan our spirit into flame. In these verses Paul said, "For which cause I remind you to fan into flame the gift of God, which is in you through the laying on of my hands. For God has not given us a spirit of cowardice, but of power and of love and of sober-mindedness." Some might think that these verses do not say that we should fan our spirit but that we should fan our gift. But if you get into these verses, you will see that the fanning of our gift into flame is the fanning of our spirit into flame. Paul tells us in verse 6 to "fan into flame the gift of God." Then in verse 7 he says, "For God has not given us a spirit...." Our God-given spirit is what we must fan into flame. We have to fan our spirit.

We have to know the background of 2 Timothy to appreciate Paul's word here. Paul wrote this book during a difficult time for his spiritual son Timothy. Paul was in prison in Rome. Furthermore, all those in Asia had forsaken Paul's ministry (v. 15). The churches in Asia were the main churches raised up through Paul's ministry, but they forsook him. Timothy was there among them. If you were Timothy, how would you face the situation? People could have said to Timothy, "Why are you still following Paul? All the saints in Asia have forsaken him. Also, if God were really with him, He would rescue him from the prison in Rome." No doubt, Timothy was discouraged. Otherwise, Paul would not have said, "For which cause I remind you...." Timothy was discouraged and had to be reminded. Paul knew Timothy was down and he sympathized with him. He reminded Timothy that there was still a small fire within him which he needed to fan into flame.

At times you may suffer to such an extent that you may begin to doubt God and doubt your salvation. But regardless of how much you doubt, one thing is within you which you cannot deny—your spirit. You are not like a beast. You have a spirit. This spirit is a trouble to Satan. Regardless of how much work Satan has done and is still doing, there is one thing within that he cannot touch—our spirit. We need to fan our spirit into flame.

We may say that the gift of God which we must fan into flame is a spiritual gift. But without our spirit, how could we have the gift? The spiritual gift is in our spirit. There is fire in our regenerated spirit, which is indwelt by the Holy Spirit. Actually, we may say that our spirit is the fire.

A small fire that is fanned into flame can turn into a great fire. A forest fire is an example of this. The wind fans the small fire into a great fire. If something were burning within a house, and you wanted to fan that fire, you would open the window or the door. The wind would cause the fire to burn into a flame. The easiest way for you to fan your spirit is to open up your mouth.

If you want to fan your spirit into flame, you need to open up your mouth, open up your heart, and open up your spirit. You need to open these three layers of your being. You have to use your mouth to say, "O Lord Jesus." But then you have to go deeper by using your mouth with your heart to say, "O Lord Jesus." Then you need to go even deeper by using your mouth with your heart and with your spirit to say, "O Lord Jesus." This is to open up your spirit from deep within. Then the fire burns. If you are down, you should call, "O Lord Jesus" again and again from deep within with the exercise of your spirit. Then you will be up.

Paul wrote 2 Timothy 1:6-7 according to his experience. He reminded Timothy to fan into flame the gift of God within him. Then he said that God has not given us a spirit of cowardice. Instead, God has given us a spirit in the center of our being surrounded by the three parts of the soul—the will, the emotion, and the mind. The spirit given to us by God is of power, of love, and of sobermindedness. Power belongs to our will. Love belongs to our emotion. Sobermindedness belongs to our mind. God has given us a spirit of these three things. Our will should be strong, full of power; our emotion should be loving, full of love; and our mind should be sober, full of sobermindedness.

According to the divine revelation, God does not give us a spirit of cowardice, but a spirit of power. That means your spirit is connected to your will, which is powerful. So whenever you exercise your spirit, you have to realize that your will is involved. Our spirit is surrounded not only by the powerful will but also by the loving emotion and by the sober mind. That means your mind should not be cloudy or foggy, but very clear, very sober.

Paul had the revelation of this and also the experience. Verses 6 and 7 of 2 Timothy 1 are marvelous. These verses show us that we saved ones have the capital to live the Christian life and the church life. This capital is the God-given spirit. This God-given spirit, according to God's ordination, is surrounded by the power of our will, by the love of our emotion, and by the sobermindedness of our mind. These three helpers are surrounding our spirit, not to depress us, but rather to uplift us and help us.

We have to exercise such a God-given spirit. The capital for a person to run in a race is his God-created legs. Without God creating two legs for you, how could you run? You have no capital to run. In like manner, if God did not give us a spirit, we would not have the capital to run the Christian race. But today we have a great account, a great deposit in the bank. We have a God-given spirit. As long as we have the God-given spirit, we have power, love, and a sober mind with a clear sky.

To say that we have the capital means that we have the capacity. We can do things because we have the capacity of power. We should not say that we do not love people, because we have the capacity of love. We should not say that we are in darkness, because we have the capacity of sobermindedness with a clear sky. We should declare, "My sky is not cloudy; my sky is clear," because this is our capacity.

Quite often we are cheated and deceived by the enemy. We say that we are weak and cloudy. But when we say we are weak, we are weak. When we say we are cloudy, we are cloudy. On the other hand, when we say we are strong, we are strong. When we say we are clear, we are clear. When we say what we are, that is what we are. Do not say you are weak. If you say you are weak, weakness is with you. But if you say you are strong, strength is with you. We can say we are strong because we have the capacity. We have the capital. God gave us, not a spirit of cowardice but a spirit of power, of love, and of sobermindedness. We should declare this and claim this. Then we will have it. This is our portion. This is our legal, God-appointed lot, which has been allotted to us by God.

Sometimes in the past, I felt down as I was preparing to speak for the Lord. It seemed that I had nothing to speak. But at that juncture I prayed. In my prayer I realized that this was a cheating. Actually, I was not weak and I did have something. There were times when I stepped up to the podium to speak without knowing what I was going to speak. When I was asking the saints to open their Bibles to read some verses, I did not know what we would read until that very moment. After we read these verses, the message came to me. Quite often such a message is more living, more powerful, and full of more impact and supply than other messages.

I am sharing this to point out that you should not listen to what you feel or what you think. What you feel and what you think are altogether a lie, a falsehood. Christians should not believe that. We should always believe and declare and claim that we are strong. We are full of love. We can love our enemies. We are well able to love everybody. We are very clear. Our sky is crystal clear. You have to believe because you have this capital. This is your capacity. You should claim and declare, "I am strong! I am loving! I am clear!" You are blessed if you say this. This is the way to exercise your spirit. This is to fan your spirit into flame. Then you will pray. The more you pray, the more you are fanning, and the more burning there will be within you.

Whenever there is the fanning, there is always a battle with Satan. While the fanning of a fire is going on, the fire department is fighting to quench the fire. This is an illustration of Satan trying to quench the fire being fanned within us. Today there are many things that are like cold water, trying to quench our inner flame. Sometimes a telephone call comes with bad news. Then someone comes to you with more bad news. Things will happen in our environment which can quench us. At that time, we have to fight. We have to declare the facts. We have to fan our spirit into flame. Then we will be the highest persons, the super persons.

II. TO SET OUR MIND ON THE SPIRIT

After you fan your spirit into flame, learn to practice another thing. Always manage your mind. Do not let your mind be a "wild horse." The mind is the great part of the soul, and the soul is in between our outward flesh and our inward spirit. Romans 8:6 says, "The mind set on the flesh is death, but the mind set on the spirit is life and peace." After fanning our spirit into flame, we must learn to set our mind on the spirit. Our mind is very "talkative." The mind speaks to us everywhere at all times. If we do not control our mind, we can wander in our imagination all over the globe within a short time. We can dream in our mind even during the day. This is why we must direct our mind to the spirit. When we do this, we will sing to the Lord, praise the Lord, or speak forth the Lord.

It is easy for the husband and the wife to commit sins because when they are with each other, they do not set their mind on the spirit. Before other people, they will be restricted in what they say. But when they are together, they may feel free to gossip about others or speak negatively about the church. At that time they are in death because they are setting their mind upon the flesh. But we have to learn to fan our spirit into flame and to control our mind. Do not let the mind be set upon the flesh, but direct it to be set upon the spirit. This habit has to be built up in us. To set our mind on the flesh is death. To set our mind on the spirit is life and peace.

III. TO DISCERN OUR SPIRIT FROM OUR SOUL

In Hebrews 4:12 the word *discern* is used. It says that the word of God can divide our soul from our spirit and is able to *discern* the thoughts and intentions of the heart. Quite often our thoughts are deceiving. But if we exercise our spirit, there is a discernment that our thoughts are evil, because behind our thoughts there is an evil intention. To discern the thoughts and intents of the heart equals the dividing of the soul from the spirit. All the time you have to keep your spirit separate from your soul. The enemy's strategy is always to mix our spirit up with our soul. In today's world nearly everyone is in a mixed situation. They mix up their spirit with their soul. Whenever such mixing is there, the spirit loses and the soul wins.

Before a brother begins to talk to his wife about another brother, he has to consider, "Is this of my spirit or of my soul?" If it is of his soul, what he says will be either gossip or criticism. If it is of his spirit, what he says will be something led by the Lord. This shows that we have to discern our spirit from our soul. We, the ones who are seeking after Christ, must learn to fan our spirit into flame, to set our mind on the spirit, and also to discern our spirit from our soul.

Actually, our person, our being, is quite complicated. We are not so simple, because we have three parts. We have the flesh which is bad, the spirit which is good, and the soul which is in between. We should always follow our spirit and walk in all things according to our spirit. This is according to Romans 8:4. We should always be on the alert to discern anything that is not of the spirit but of the soul. Then we will remain in the spirit all the time. This is to exercise, to use, to employ, our spirit.

Our God-given spirit is our capital and our capacity. We have to use our spirit, to employ our spirit, and to exercise our spirit by fanning it into flame, by setting our mind upon it, and by discerning it from our soul. Of course, it is easy to know what is of the flesh and what is of the spirit; but quite often it is a very mixed-up situation between what is of the soul and what is of the spirit. This is why we have to discern.

When we get into these points, we can realize that our Christian walk is a very fine walk. If we are going to walk according to our spirit, we must learn not to do things too fast or to say things too quickly. It is safe to wait awhile. I have had this experience in writing answers to letters. Sometimes I will write a letter and then keep it for another day before I mail it. The next day a new thought might come to me to include in that letter or I may realize that I said something wrong. To wait in this way helps us to walk according to our spirit.

The battle in the Christian life is always there. Even within us there is a battle between the spirit and the flesh and even the more between the spirit and the soul. So we have to exercise our spirit, to use our spirit, that is, to fan our spirit into flame. Then we should learn how to control our mind by setting our mind upon our spirit. We should also always discern what is of the spirit and what is of the soul. If something is not of the spirit, we do not want to say it or do it. This is to use, to exercise, our spirit. I hope we will practice using our spirit until we build up a strong habit of exercising our spirit.

CHAPTER NINE

THE SPIRIT'S WORK ON AND IN
THE BELIEVERS

(1)

Scripture Reading: 1 Pet. 1:2; Luke 15:8-9; John 16:8-11; Luke 15:18-24

OUTLINE

I. Sanctifying the God-chosen people before they repent and believe—1 Pet. 1:2:
   A. Seeking them carefully by enlightening them until finding them—Luke 15:8-9.
   B. Convicting them—John 16:8-11:
      1. Concerning sin in Adam, not believing into Christ—v. 9.
      2. Concerning righteousness in Christ in His resurrection—v. 10.
      3. Concerning judgment with Satan unto eternal perdition—v. 11.
   C. Leading them to:
      1. Repent unto God—Luke 15:18-21.
      2. Receive Christ as their life supply—Luke 15:22-24.

Beginning in this message we want to study, to investigate, the Spirit's work on and in the believers.

I. SANCTIFYING THE GOD-CHOSEN PEOPLE BEFORE THEY REPENT AND BELIEVE

The first work the Spirit has done with us is to sanctify us. The Spirit sanctifies the God-chosen people before they repent and believe (1 Pet. 1:2). Not many Christians realize this. *Lord, right now sanctify Aunt Colette*

The Bible also reveals that sanctification is after justification. First, God justified us by our believing in Christ. Then God continues to work on us by sanctifying us. The book of Romans speaks of this aspect of sanctification. The first section of the book of Romans, from 1:18 through 3:20, is on God's condemnation. The second section, from 3:21 through 5:11, is on God's justification. Then the third section, from 5:12 through 8:13, is on sanctification. This is the very crucial section of the book of Romans. Romans 5 is "in Adam," Romans 6 is "in Christ," Romans 7 is "in the flesh," and Romans 8 is "in the Spirit." Romans 6:19 and 22 refer to the sanctification that takes place after our justification.

But we also need to see that God sanctifies His chosen people even before they repent and believe. First Peter 1:2 says, "Chosen according to the foreknowledge of God the Father in the sanctification of the Spirit unto obedience and the sprinkling of the blood of Jesus Christ." This is a crucial verse in the New Testament. This verse reveals that there is another step of the Spirit's sanctification before our repentance.

Peter begins with God's choosing, God's selection, in eternity. God knew us in eternity. Before we were born, before we were created, before Adam was created, and even before the universe was created, God foreknew us. According to God's foreknowledge, He chose us. He was like a person coming to a supermarket, looking around at all the items, and choosing the ones that he liked. He chose each one of us in this way. It would be good to circle the word *chosen* in our Bible. How wonderful it is that we have been chosen according to our Father's foreknowledge!

This verse goes on to say that we were chosen in the sanctification of the Spirit. The phrase *in the sanctification of the Spirit* functions as an adverb to modify the verb *chosen*. According to the grammar, this is one thing. If I say, "I speak with my mouth," this is one thing. *With my mouth* modifies the verb *speak*. God did not choose *and* sanctify us, but He chose us *in* the sanctification of the Spirit. This is also one thing and one action. We were chosen in eternity past, but we were sanctified in time. But 1 Peter 1:2 links eternity with time. In God, there is no time element. God chose us and He did it in the sanctification of the Spirit. God's choosing and the Spirit's sanctification are one action.

Then 1 Peter 1:2 says that God's choosing us in the sanctification of the Spirit was "unto obedience and the sprinkling of the blood of Jesus Christ." *Obedience* in the New Testament implies two things. First, our obedience to God implies our repentance. Then it implies our faith. We were away from God. We were His enemies. Then the Spirit came to work on us, and this was *unto* something. *Unto* here means "resulting in." So the Spirit's sanctification results in our repentance and faith. These two things added together are our obedience. Sanctification of the Spirit is unto the obedience of repentance and believing. The real obedience to God is to repent to God and believe into the Lord Jesus.

Following our obedience, we experience "the sprinkling of the blood of Jesus Christ." The sprinkling of the blood of Christ came upon us, not before our repentance but after our faith. God's choosing is first, and this was in the Spirit's sanctification. This resulted in obedience, consisting of repentance and faith. Then we are ready to receive God's redemption, and the first step of God's redemption is for Him to sprinkle us with His blood. Without the sprinkling, the washing, of the blood, there is no way for God to save us.

Obedience is on our side, but choosing in sanctification is on God's side. God chose us in eternity, but the working out of the sentence in 1 Peter 1:2 is not finished yet. We were chosen in eternity in the sanctification of the Spirit in time, and this sanctification issues in our repentance and faith, which is our obedience. He was ready from eternity to redeem us, but we were not ready. Then we received His Spirit's sanctification, and that resulted in our repentance and faith in God's Son, Jesus Christ. Now we are ready to receive God's salvation. The first thing in His salvation is to sprinkle us with the blood of the Second of the Trinity. So we get washed, forgiven, justified, and reconciled to God. Thus, we can see that before our repentance and faith there was the sanctification by the Spirit. First Peter 1:2 shows that the sprinkling of the blood follows the sanctification of the Spirit.

I hope this brief fellowship shows us the way to study the Word. Even a small preposition in the Bible needs our study. First Peter 1:2 does not say that God chose us *through* but *in* the sanctification of the Spirit. God's choosing could not be practiced without the Spirit's sanctifying. It is the sanctifying of the Spirit that carries out God's choosing.

A. Seeking Them Carefully by Enlightening Them until Finding Them

Now we need to consider what the Spirit did when He sanctified us. The sanctifying of the Spirit before our repentance is recorded in the Bible in a very detailed way. But the Bible is like a big jigsaw puzzle. It does not give you every part of the picture in a gathered way, but the pieces are scattered throughout it. We have to learn how to put the pieces together to see a complete picture.

Luke 15:8-9 says, "Or what woman having ten silver coins, if she loses one silver coin, does not light a lamp and sweep the house and seek carefully until she finds it? And when she finds it, she calls together her friends and neighbors, saying, Rejoice with me, for I have found the coin which I lost." This portion of the Word gives us a picture of the Spirit's sanctifying work. We need to notice the words *seek* and *finds*. The woman, signifying the Spirit, seeks the lost silver coin carefully until she finds it.

In Luke 15 the Lord gave us three parables: the parable of a good shepherd finding the lost sheep; the parable of a fine woman seeking for her lost treasure; and the parable of a loving father expecting his prodigal son to come back. When we get into the significance of this chapter, we can realize

that this surely refers to the Triune God. The Father is wait-
ing lovingly to receive the sinners back to Himself, but how
could they come back? First, the Son is the good Shepherd
taking care of the lost sinners, and then the Spirit is working.

We saved sinners were God's chosen people. The coin,
before being lost, was the treasure of the woman. The woman
signifies the Spirit. The Spirit who is working on us and in us
is not like a tiger or even a man. The Spirit works like a sister,
a woman. The sisters are finer and sweeter than the brothers.
They were born that way. Thank the Lord that the Spirit is
the Woman, the Lord is the Shepherd, and God is the Father.
The Father with the Shepherd and the Woman work together
in love to save fallen sinners. This is detailed in the divine
revelation.

The Spirit as a woman came to the lost sinners. They are
God's chosen people. They were once in God's hand as His
treasure, His coins. Even before we were lost, we were trea-
sures in the Lord's hand. Then one day we became lost. But in
eternity God predestinated us to bring us back to Himself.
The first blessing that God rendered to us in eternity past
was His choosing us unto sanctification. Ephesians 1:4 says,
"He chose us in Him before the foundation of the world to be
holy...." He has chosen us to be holy. This is unto sanctification. Our being made holy began when the Spirit as the
woman came to seek us, to bring us back to God unto His
holiness.

In time the Spirit as the woman came to seek us, not just
to find us. She came to seek carefully for the lost coin. I like
the word *carefully*. Who does this careful work? The sanctifying Spirit of God. The Spirit is almighty, all-capable, and
omnipotent, but She (I use the female pronoun here) needs to
seek carefully. This is because we were very complicated
before we were saved. It was not easy for the Spirit to find us.
So the woman, the Spirit, came to seek for us carefully by
lighting a lamp. The lamp here signifies the word of God (Psa.
119:105, 130). One day when we heard the gospel, some of the
words in the Bible began to shine in us. In my youth I got to
know John 3:16. But for many years that did not work on me.
One day, however, the seeking Spirit caused this verse to

shine within me. The word of God is a lamp used by the Spirit to illuminate and expose the sinner's position and condition that he may repent.

The Spirit as a woman lit a lamp, and then she swept the house. To sweep the house is to search and cleanse the sinner's inward parts. The Spirit who sought us lit the word and swept within us, in our inner being, until she found us. To find is to get. Thus, the Spirit is a woman coming to seek us by lighting the word and sweeping within us, in our inner being, until she gets us. The word began to shine within us while the Spirit was sweeping to clear away all the dirt from within us. She did this until she got us. This is the sanctifying of the Spirit. When we were in the world, among a heap of sinners, the Spirit came to seek us, to visit us, to seek us out carefully by lighting God's word of life. At the same time, she was sweeping within us to clear away all the dirt within us. Then we started to repent.

B. Convicting Them

Another portion of the Word that shows the sanctifying Spirit is John 16:8-11. These verses say, "And when He comes, He will convict the world concerning sin and concerning righteousness and concerning judgment: concerning sin, because they do not believe into Me; and concerning righteousness, because I am going to the Father and you no longer behold Me; and concerning judgment, because the ruler of this world has been judged." Luke 15:8-9 plus John 16:8-11 are on the sanctifying Spirit. This sanctifying of the Spirit includes the Spirit's seeking us and convicting us. Her seeking was for her convicting. The Spirit came to us to sanctify us unto God, to separate us unto God, first by seeking us carefully and second by convicting us prevailingly. The Spirit convicts us concerning sin, concerning righteousness, and concerning judgment. These three items are big subjects in the New Testament.

1. Concerning Sin in Adam

First, the Spirit convicts the world concerning sin in Adam because they do not believe into Christ (John 16:9). Romans

5:12 says that sin entered into the world, into the people of the earth, through Adam. Adam was a big entry for sin to come in to all his descendants. We need to repent of the sin in Adam and believe into Christ. The sin which came into us from Adam causes us not to believe into Christ. To be born in Adam and not believe into Christ makes us sinners. We are companions of sin. We belong to sin. Sin is our kingdom, our realm, our field. We were in sin, in Adam, in our not believing into Christ. The Spirit convicts us that we are in Adam and will not believe into Christ. This is the first aspect of His convicting.

2. Concerning Righteousness
in Christ in His Resurrection

Then the Spirit convicts us concerning righteousness in Christ in His resurrection (John 16:10). Sin is in Adam. Righteousness is in Christ. Without Christ, there is no righteousness. On the whole earth, in the whole universe righteousness is in Christ, and He is God's righteousness given to us as our righteousness (1 Cor. 1:30). This is altogether in His resurrection. Romans 4:25 says Christ was resurrected for our justification, for our righteousness. If Christ only died on the cross and still remained in the tomb, there would be no righteousness and we could never be made righteous. Justification, to make Christ our righteousness, is through His resurrection.

We need to remember that Luke 15 was the Lord's parable, and John 16 was the Lord's teaching. Both came out of the mouth of the Lord Jesus, the One who is wisdom. Only Christ could have given us the parable in Luke 15. And only He could have given us the teaching in John 16. The parable in Luke 15 has the details. The teaching in John 16 has the crucial major points—sin, righteousness, and judgment. Sin as we have seen is in Adam, causing us not to believe. Not believing into Christ is the real sin before God. Then righteousness is in Christ. He died for our sins, and He was buried. Then He rose up for us to have Him as our righteousness, for us to be justified by God with Him as our righteousness.

3. Concerning Judgment with Satan
unto Eternal Perdition

The Spirit also convicts the world concerning judgment with Satan unto eternal perdition (v. 11). Between God and man, there are three crucial things—sin, righteousness, and judgment. As we have seen, sin came from Adam and righteousness is of Christ. Surely judgment is for the evil one, Satan (Matt. 25:41). In this whole universe, Adam, Christ, and Satan are the three biggest roles. We were born in Adam, in sin. If we believe into Christ, we receive Him as our righteousness. If not, we will go with Satan to share his judgment in the lake of fire. While the Spirit is seeking us out, He convicts us concerning this sin, concerning this righteousness, and concerning this judgment.

We need to learn these things because we are going out to contact people. We can read Luke 15:8 to the ones for whom we are caring to show them the Spirit's seeking. Then we can read John 16:8-11 to them to show them the Spirit's convicting. I believe every contact would be happy to hear this. This shows that in order to be effective in our contact with people, we must study the Bible. We can present some verses from the Bible to them with the proper definition. Then we will gain them. We should learn how to preach these things so that the seeking Spirit can light our words to make them shine. Then others will be convicted and repent.

C. Leading Them to:

1. Repent unto God

In Luke 15 there are the Spirit's seeking and the Spirit's stirring up to lead us to God the Father. The third parable in Luke 15 is concerning a father receiving his son. Verses 18 through 21 tell us what happened when the prodigal son decided to return. "I will rise up and go to my father, and I will say to him, Father, I have sinned against heaven and before you. I am no longer worthy to be called your son; make me like one of your hired servants. And he rose up and came to his own father. But while he was still a long way off, his father saw him and was moved with compassion, and he ran and fell on his neck and kissed him affectionately. And the son said to him, Father, I have sinned against heaven and before you; I am no longer worthy to be called your son."

The prodigal son suddenly said that he would rise up and go to his father. As sons we rose up and came to our Father because we were stirred up by the seeking and convicting Spirit. For the son to say, "Father, I have sinned," is for him to make a confession following his repentance. When he said that he would be as one of his father's hired servants, this meant that he wanted to work for his father to gain his father's favor. Once a fallen sinner has repented, he thinks of working for God or of serving God to obtain His favor, not knowing that this thought is against God's love and grace and is an insult to His heart and intent.

2. Receive Christ as Their Life Supply

The father's response to his son is seen in verses 22 through 24. "But the father said to his slaves, Bring out quickly the best robe and put it on him, and put a ring on his hand and sandals on his feet. And bring the fattened calf; slaughter it, and let us eat and be merry, because this son of mine was dead and lives again; he was lost and has been found. And they began to be merry." The son came back as a poor, pitiful prodigal, but the father gave him three things: a robe, a ring, and sandals. The father clothed his son with the best robe to cover him. This robe signifies Christ as our righteousness for our justification (Jer. 23:6; 1 Cor. 1:30; cf. Isa. 61:10; Zech. 3:4). The ring signifies the sealing Spirit as the God-given seal upon the accepted believer (Eph. 1:13). If someone is wearing a gold ring, he must have a lot of money. The ring on the son's finger was a mark that he had become rich. The sandals signify the power of God's salvation to separate the believers from the dirty earth.

Now he was no longer a poor prodigal, but a rich young man. He was now qualified to enter the father's house, but he needed something to eat. He had been eating the carob pods which the hogs were eating (Luke 15:16) and he had walked quite a distance to his father's house without eating anything. He was clothed with a robe, marked with a ring, and separated from the earth with a pair of shoes, but his stomach surely was crying out for food. So the father told his slaves to kill the fattened calf for his son's enjoyment (v. 23). This signifies the rich Christ (Eph. 3:8), killed on the cross for the believers' enjoyment. After we are justified by God with Christ, we receive Christ as our satisfaction, as our supply, as the fattened calf.

Thus, Christ here is first a robe and then the fattened calf. In resurrection He has become our food, our life supply. This is the result of the seeking and convicting of the Spirit. The seeking and convicting of the Spirit issue in our obedience, in our repentance and faith. Eventually, we receive Christ outwardly as our righteousness and inwardly as our life and life supply. This is the sanctification of the Spirit, the first step of God's salvation.

CHAPTER TEN

THE SPIRIT'S WORK ON AND IN
THE BELIEVERS

(2)

Scripture Reading: John 3:5-6, 8; 1:12-13; 3:6; 1 Pet. 1:3; Titus 3:5

OUTLINE

II. Regenerating the convicted and believing believers—John 3:5-6, 8:
  A. Begetting them to be the children of God—John 1:12-13:
    1. In their spirit—John 3:6.
    2. Through the resurrection of Christ—1 Pet. 1:3.
    3. Into the kingdom of God—John 3:5.
  B. Washing away the filthiness of the old nature of their old man—Titus 3:5:
    1. Putting off their old man and putting on the new.
    2. Reconditioning their state from the old creation to the new.

In the previous message, we saw the Spirit's work in sanctifying the God-chosen people before they repent and believe. In this message we want to see the Spirit's work in regenerating the convicted and believing believers (John 3:5-6, 8).

I hope that we would all learn to know the thought of the Bible. When a person writes something, his thought is in his writing. We need to know the Lord's thought in the Scriptures. In reading 1 Peter 1:2 and 3, we can see not only the thought of Peter but also the thought of the inspiring Spirit. These verses say, "Chosen according to the foreknowledge of God the Father in the sanctification of the Spirit unto obedience and the sprinkling of the blood of Jesus Christ: Grace to you and peace be multiplied. Blessed be the God and Father of our Lord Jesus Christ, who according to His great mercy has regenerated us unto a living hope through the resurrection of Jesus Christ from the dead."

The main thought in these two verses is embodied in three crucial words: *chosen, sanctification,* and *regenerated.* God chose us in eternity past. Then in time the Spirit came to sanctify us. God's choosing is in the Spirit's sanctification. Now we need to consider the purpose of God's choosing and of the Spirit's sanctifying. God's choosing and the Spirit's sanctifying do not have two goals. They have only one goal. They are on the same line, the same road. It is not that God takes one way, and the Spirit takes another way. They are taking one way. God started the way to choose us, and the Spirit follows in the same way, in the same line, to sanctify us. God's choosing and sanctifying are for the purpose of producing sons. God's intention is to have many sons.

God can have many sons not by adoption but by begetting. John 3:3 says that we must be "born anew." This is not just generating but regenerating. In God's economy, God must first have man in His creation. His creation of man was a kind of bringing forth, a kind of begetting. How can we prove that God's creation was God's begetting? Luke 3:38 says, "Adam, the son of God." This is a strong verse to prove that God's creation was a kind of begetting. Adam was created by God (Gen. 5:1-2), and God was his origin. God did not breathe His breath of life into the plants, the fish, the birds, or the cattle. In God's creation, God breathed the breath of life only into Adam (Gen. 2:7). Luke considered that this was God's begetting. That was humankind's first birth.

Charles Wesley's hymn "Hark! The Herald Angels Sing" (*Hymns,* #84) is of a very high standard. I would like to point out stanza 3 of this hymn, which says, "Born to raise the sons of earth; / Born to give them second birth." God's economy needs man to go through two births. He receives a human life in his first birth. Then he has to go through another birth, the second birth. This birth is for him to receive the divine life. God intended that man would have two lives—the human life and the divine life. In order to do this, God must have a prototype, a model. So He Himself became incarnated to be the prototype.

At one time God merely had the divine life, not the human life. But He had the intention that mankind would have two lives, the human and the divine. Therefore, He Himself had to be a prototype. He set up a model by becoming incarnated. God with the divine life came into humanity that He might have the human life. Thus, on this earth there was a unique model, the God-man. Today this prototype has been duplicated in mass production because in resurrection He has become the Firstborn among many brothers (Rom. 8:29).

After man was made by God, God saw what He had made and used the words *very good* to describe it (Gen. 1:31). But this very good man became fallen. Most people think that if Adam had not fallen, he and we would not have needed to be regenerated, but this is absolutely wrong. Even if man had never fallen, he would still have needed to be reborn. The God-created man needed to be reborn of God, not just to have God's breath of life, but to have God's life itself. Man needed regeneration even if man had never fallen. God in His economy planned it this way.

The Old Testament tells us that Saul was anointed by God and got another heart (1 Sam. 10:9). A new heart is obviously something new, but another heart may still be the old heart. Saul did not have something new. God created an old man, and this old man should have a transformation, a change from the old to the new. The old man was human; the new man is divine. We all have to see this. Today we are wonderful persons because we have been regenerated with God's divine life. We are now both divine and human. When God was incarnated, He could say, "I am a God-man." Now that we have been regenerated, we can say, "I am a man-God." The only difference is this: He had the divine life first. Then He received the human life. We had the human life first. Then we received the divine life. Eventually, God has two lives with two natures, and we are the same.

Christ was born to give us a second birth, that is, to make us God in His life and nature, but not in His Godhead. God was made a man, and we men are being made God, but without the Godhead. There is a two-way traffic. He comes with divinity to enter into humanity, and we go with humanity to enter into divinity. This is the significance of regeneration according to the blueprint, the plan, of God. By His mercy God has really shown us His plan, His economy. The main line we have seen in God's plan is that God intended to be a man. This is His hobby, His heart's desire. What does God want? God wants to get a man for Him to be one with man. This is the reason why He loves man. So first, He created a man, and this creation of man can be considered as a begetting of man. Four thousand years later, He came to be a man. He was not separate from man, but He became a man in union with man. He entered into man.

God came to be a man to give us a second birth. God can do everything, but if He had not become a man, He could not regenerate man. He must have the qualification of being God and man. He became a man in His incarnation to put on humanity, and this part of Him, the human part, was not divine. While He was on this earth for thirty-three and a half years, He was part divine and part human. In His incarnation He put on man. Then He took the second step to die and resurrect. In resurrection He "sonized" His human part, making this human part divine.

Obviously, we were born human. Then God as the prototype came into us as the divine One. Now it will take our whole life for Him to transform our humanity into something divine. This transformation is the process of "sonizing" us. In one sense, we are now the sons of God because we have been begotten of God with His life. But in our attitude, actions, and behavior we may appear as the sons of beggars. This shows that in another sense, we do not appear to be the sons of God. We should say, "I am a son of God in life and nature, but not yet fully in constitution and appearance. I am being transformed day by day." Now we are under God's transformation. To transform us is to sonize us. This is God's work in us every day.

God created man in a way that he needs a wife as a helpmate to match him. But the highest purpose in God's giving a wife to a brother is to give him trouble so that he can be transformed. Many times it is the wife who troubles the husband the most and the husband who troubles the wife the most. God uses this situation to transform the husband and the wife. The wives perfect the husbands, and the husbands perfect the wives. Even our children become helpers to us in the process of transformation. We also need a job in order to live, and our job is used by the Lord to transform us. All of our daily necessities are troubles. People like to have a car, but the car becomes a trouble. People like to have computers, but computers also become a trouble to them. These troubles are ordained by God so that we can be transformed.

In my earlier ministry, I told people that our circumstances and environment are ordained by God for our transformation. But I did not realize as much as I do today. Everything we need becomes a trouble. God ordained these things so that we could be sonized, transformed.

Transformation is a continuation of regeneration. We have been regenerated and we are a new man, but the process does not stop there. The butterfly does not come out of the cocoon overnight. It comes out slowly. Sanctification, renewing, and transformation are all a continuation of regeneration to make us a new man with the divine and human natures. Eventually, 1 John 3 says that when He comes, we will see Him, and at that time we will be the same as He is (v. 2).

God has only one way to go in this whole universe. This is the way of His economy to gain many sons for His expression.

The first step God took was His choosing. Ephesians 1 tells us that God's choosing was for His sanctification, for us to be holy (v. 4). God chose us in eternity, predestinating us unto sonship (v. 5). He chose us with an intention to get sons. After His choosing, He came as the Spirit to sanctify us, to separate us, from the heap of common people. The Spirit came to seek us, to enlighten us, to find us, and to get us (Luke 15:8-9). He worked to convict us (John 16:8), causing us to repent and stirring up our heart that we might have the desire to go to God. Then we became believers.

After He sanctified us as the Spirit, He regenerated us. First Peter 1:2 speaks of God's choosing and the Spirit's sanctifying. Then verse 3 says that following His sanctification, He regenerated us through the resurrection of Christ. Regeneration is the step following the Spirit's sanctification. First, God chose us; then God the Spirit came to sanctify us; and sanctification is for sonizing, which begins with the Spirit regenerating us.

For us to study the work of the Spirit on and in the believers is for us to study the real Christian life. Soon after I was regenerated, I wanted to know the real significance of regeneration. It was very difficult to find anyone who taught this. Eventually, I read a book by T. Austin-Sparks which really helped me. In that book he spoke a very precious word. He said that regeneration is to have God's life, as another life, in addition to your human life. This is the proper definition and significance of regeneration. For the Lord to give us a second birth means that He gave us another life, a second life, the divine life.

II. REGENERATING THE CONVICTED
AND BELIEVING BELIEVERS

The Spirit works to regenerate the convicted and believing believers (John 3:5-6, 8).

A. Begetting Them to Be the Children of God

According to John 1:12 and 13, those who receive Christ by believing into Him will be born of God to be God's children. Of course, this is the second birth.

1. *In Their Spirit*

John 3:6 says, "That which is born of the Spirit is spirit." Regeneration takes place in our spirit. It is accomplished in the human spirit by the Holy Spirit of God with God's life, the uncreated eternal life.

2. *Through the Resurrection of Christ*

First Peter 1:3 says that God regenerated us through the resurrection of Jesus Christ from among the dead. We need to consider why regeneration needs to be through the resurrection of Christ. God created man, but man became fallen. Through this fall Satan came in to join with man, so man became a real problem to God. Man was created by God without sin, having nothing to do with Satan. But through his fall, he became sinful. Romans 5:12 says that sin entered into man through one person, Adam. Thus, man became joined to Satan.

How could such a person of sin and of Satan be regenerated? There is the need for this person to be put to death and to be buried. Then there is the need of the divine life to raise up this dead and buried one. Who can put us all to death, bury us, and raise us up? Only the One who passed through death, was buried, and rose up. He is the qualified One. His death and resurrection are the process, the means, through which we can be made dead, buried, and resurrected to have another life. This is the procedure of our regeneration. So Christ had to put on humanity and to bring this humanity to the cross. Then He brought us into His death and burial (Rom. 6:3-4) and raised us up with Himself in His resurrection (Eph. 2:6).

Christ's resurrection was a big birth, a big delivery. Not only was Christ Jesus resurrected and begotten in that delivery (Acts 13:33). Millions also joined Him in that birth (Rom. 8:29; 1 Pet. 1:3). In resurrection Christ as the last Adam became a life-giving Spirit (1 Cor. 15:45b). Then through His resurrection, many Satan-possessed sinners were all regenerated. We need such a revelation. We need a revelation to see that we were created by God, yet we became fallen, involved with sin and joined with Satan. So we became a kind of trinity—fallen man with sin and Satan. Yet God chose us. Then He regenerated us by bringing us into death and burial and raising us up in Christ's resurrection. Through Christ's resurrection we became reborn. We had a second birth and received another life with another nature, both divine.

In the divine viewpoint, our regeneration transpired about two thousand years ago in Christ's resurrection. It transpired before our first birth. With God there is no time element. First, He created man and then He joined Himself to man. Later, the Spirit came to us to bring Him, the One who passed through death, burial, and resurrection, into us to make His history our experience, to make us one with Him, fully identical to Him. So we died, we were buried, and we rose up to be a regenerated new man, a new man with a second birth.

3. Into the Kingdom of God

The Lord Jesus said that if you are not born anew, you cannot enter into the kingdom of God (John 3:5). Man cannot enter into the animal kingdom to fellowship with the animals and understand them, because man was not born with the animal life. The animals were born into the animal kingdom. God also has a kingdom. We cannot understand the things of God if we are not in His kingdom. The only way to enter into His kingdom is to be born into it. In our first birth, we were born into the human kingdom. Only man knows the things of man in the human kingdom. The animals cannot know us or understand us. In like manner, how can we understand the things of God in the kingdom of God? The only way is to be born into His kingdom with His life. Now we have been born into the kingdom of God, so we can know God. According to Genesis 1, all of the animals were created according to their kind. But we men were created by God according to God's kind. A "kind" is a kingdom. Later, we were reborn into God's kingdom, into His kind.

B. Washing Away the Filthiness of the Old Nature of Their Old Man

Titus 3:5 speaks of the washing of regeneration. Regeneration is a washing. It washes away the filthiness of the old nature of our old man. This washing away is to put off our old man and put on the new man. It is also a kind of reconditioning. We all have been regenerated, reconditioned, with the divine life. Regeneration is very deep. I like this word *recondition*. Charles Wesley used the word *reinstate* in stanza 4 of hymn #84—"Reinstate us in Thy love." We lost our state, our position, so we needed to be reinstated. But we also needed to be reconditioned. Our nature, our essence, and our entire being needed to be reconditioned. Nothing can do this except regeneration. To be regenerated is to be reborn, reconditioned, with the divine life.

CHAPTER ELEVEN

THE SPIRIT'S WORK ON AND IN
THE BELIEVERS

(3)

THE SPIRIT'S DISPOSITIONAL SANCTIFICATION

Scripture Reading: 1 Pet. 1:2; Heb. 13:12; 9:13-14; 10:29; Rom.
15:16b; 6:19, 22; Titus 3:5; Rom. 12:2b; 2 Cor. 4:16; 3:18;
1 Thes. 5:23; Eph. 1:4-5

OUTLINE

I. The three aspects of the sanctification in the Scriptures:
   A. The Spirit's sanctification in seeking the God-chosen people before their repentance—1 Pet. 1:2.
   B. The sanctification by the blood of Christ at the time of the believers' believing—Heb. 13:12; 9:13-14; 10:29.
   C. The Spirit's dispositional sanctification in the believers' full course of their Christian life—Rom. 15:16b; 6:19, 22.

II. The essential works of the Spirit's dispositional sanctification:
   A. To continue the ongoing work of the believers' regeneration.
   B. To carry out the renewing of the believers as God's new creation—Titus 3:5; Rom. 12:2b; 2 Cor. 4:16.
   C. To perform the Lord's transformation of the believers—2 Cor. 3:18; Rom. 12:2b.
   D. To consummate in the believers' glorification—1 Thes. 5:23.
   E. To complete God's sonship in choosing the believers—Eph. 1:4-5.

I. THE THREE ASPECTS OF
THE SANCTIFICATION IN THE SCRIPTURES

The truth concerning sanctification has been a puzzling matter among Christian teachers throughout the years. Different teachers have had different opinions about the significance of sanctification. John Wesley thought that sanctification was sinless perfection.

We received help from the teaching of the Brethren to see that John Wesley's word was not accurate. The Brethren taught the truth concerning sanctification based upon the Lord's words in Matthew 23, where the Lord said that the gold was sanctified by the temple and that the gift, the offering, was sanctified by the altar (vv. 17, 19). Sanctification is not sinless perfection or purity, because the gold did not become more pure when it was sanctified by the temple. Its being sanctified was not related to its purity. When the gold was in the market, it was common and worldly, but the same gold in the temple became holy, sanctified. When it was sanctified by the temple unto God, that sanctification changed the position of the gold. Thus, sanctification, the Brethren said, is a matter of position.

In Matthew 23 the Lord Jesus also referred us to the sacrifices, the offerings, sanctified by the altar. In the flock a sheep is common. But when it is put on the altar, the altar sanctifies it, making it holy, unto God. So again the Brethren showed that this has nothing to do with purity or perfection. But this is to change the position of the sacrifice. The gold in the temple and the sacrifice on the altar are sanctified by changing their location from a common place to a holy place.

We accepted this teaching concerning positional sanctification because it is very scripturally based, but we were still not so satisfied that we had seen the full truth concerning sanctification. Eventually, the Lord showed us that sanctification is not so simple. There is only one sanctification, but it has three aspects. We need to see the three aspects of sanctification in the Scriptures. First, there is the Spirit's sanctification in seeking the God-chosen people before their repentance (1 Pet. 1:2). Second, there is the sanctification by the blood of Christ at the time of the believers' believing

(Heb. 13:12; 9:13-14; 10:29). Third, there is the Spirit's dispositional sanctification in the believers' full course of their Christian life (Rom. 15:16b; 6:19, 22).

Eventually, we even found out something more than this. I believe this is a final, ultimate finding. We found out that sanctification is related to God's economy, and God's economy is altogether centered on the desire of God. Ephesians 1:10 and 3:9 refer to God's economy. In eternity past without any beginning, God Himself in Christ made an economy, and the center of God's eternal economy is for God to have many sons to satisfy His heart's desire. Because God is a living person, He has a desire. In eternity past He desired to have many sons. He wanted to be a great Father with a family full of sons.

God's desire to have many sons was the center and still is the center of God's economy. The sonship is vitally important to God. First, God has a Son, and He is the only begotten Son of God (John 3:16). God was satisfied with Christ, His only begotten Son, but not in full. Eventually, God made this only begotten Son the firstborn Son among many brothers (Rom. 8:29). The only begotten Son is wonderful, but God's desire is to have many sons.

After making His economy, God started to carry out His economy in eternity past. The first step in God's carrying out of His economy was His selection. He foreknew us (1 Pet. 1:2a) and chose us in Christ before the foundation of the world (Eph. 1:4). Out of many millions of human beings, God chose you and me. He chose us by predestinating us (v. 5). To predestinate is to mark out beforehand. In eternity God saw us and chose us, so He marked us out. His choosing and marking out are actually one thing. We can illustrate this by considering the sisters' shopping at the supermarket. They may see many peaches there, but eventually they select some, mark them out, and purchase them. God chose us and marked us out in such a way in eternity.

Eventually, in time, God created man. After God's creation of Adam, Satan quickly acted to poison him. Later, in the New Testament time, God became a man. Then God as the Spirit continued to carry out His economy. He chose us and marked us out, but we became lost, so He came to seek us. This is fully unveiled in the Lord's parables in Luke 15. These parables show us how God the Father loves the son, how God the Son, for the sake of God the Father's love, came to redeem us, to gain us, to purchase us, and how the Third of the Trinity, God the Spirit, comes as a woman to do a seeking work, a finding work. She enlightened us from within and found us.

John 16 reveals that this finding Spirit convicted us concerning sin in Adam. He also convicted us concerning righteousness, causing us to realize that Christ is God's righteousness, that He wants to be our righteousness, and that we can be justified only in Him as our righteousness. Then this seeking Spirit convicted us of judgment (vv. 8-11). The universe is not without government. It is a universe in God's government, and there is a judgment. A person has the freedom to sin, but he has to realize that some day the Lord will judge him. Actually, the judgment in the lake of fire is reserved for Satan. If we do not repent of the sin that is in Adam and believe into Christ, the Son of God, as our righteousness, we will remain in sin and share the judgment of Satan for eternity (Matt. 25:41). When the Spirit convicted us concerning sin, righteousness, and judgment, we fully realized our position and our need. Then we repented and desired to turn to God and receive Christ.

This is the first aspect of the divine sanctification as revealed in 1 Peter 1:2. This aspect of the sanctification of the Spirit is before the obedience and the sprinkling of the blood of Christ. This aspect of sanctification before our repentance and believing is to find God's lost people, to bring them back, so that they can be made holy and become God's sons.

This is fully shown in Ephesians 1:4-5. In verse 4 we are told that God chose us to be holy. Then verse 5 says that in His choosing He predestinated us, marked us out, unto sonship. The word *unto* can be translated "for." God predestinated us for sonship. Thus, sanctification is a preparing step to make us sons of God. It is very much related to God's economy and to God's sonship. Sanctification does not stand alone. It is involved with God's economy from eternity and then with God's sonship in time.

From the time we were called, the sanctifying Spirit started to work for God's "sonizing," for God's sonship. This sanctifying, this sonizing, is still going on. It has been going on for about twenty centuries, and it is still not finished. We are being sanctified from within every day. We are being sonized. Sanctification is not sinless perfection, nor is it merely a positional matter. It is something that goes on and on continually to sonize God's chosen people.

The word *sonize* was invented by us to describe the process of God's sanctifying work to make us His sons in a full way. We were forced to do this. As culture progresses, there is the need of additional vocabulary to describe new things. The word *computer* was not in the dictionary a number of years ago. Even the computer itself has its own language. All the modern sciences have invented new words to describe new discoveries. Webster's dictionary is always coming up with new editions to contain the new words added because of the need of the culture. The study of the Bible is the same. The church fathers came up with the terms *Trinity* and *Triune God* to describe the fact of the person of God revealed in the Bible. They found out that there was the need to invent these terms. It is the same with us today. We have seen some deeper aspects of the truths, and we did not have the expressions to utter what we had seen. Thus, we were forced to invent new words.

What is sanctification? Sanctification is God's sonizing. When you are sanctified, you are sonized. This is based upon Ephesians 1:4-5. It is even more strongly based upon Hebrews 2:10-11, which says, "For it was fitting for Him, for whom are all things and through whom are all things, in leading many sons into glory, to make the Author of their salvation perfect through sufferings. For both He who sanctifies and those who are being sanctified are all of One...." Verse 10 speaks of bringing many sons into glory, and verse 11 speaks of the Sanctifier and the ones being sanctified. This shows that sonship is greatly dependent upon sanctification. God brings His many sons into glory by Christ's sanctifying us dispositionally, beginning from our regeneration throughout the full course of our Christian life. Sanctification is still going on because we have not yet entered into glory in full. One day we will be fully in glory. That fullness of entering into glory will be the fullness of God's sanctification.

The first aspect of sanctification was the Spirit's seeking us to bring us back unto God. We became lost in sin, but God the Spirit came to seek us out, to bring us back to God. We were like the prodigal son in Luke 15. He became like a poor beggar, and his poor situation surely did not match his rich father and did not qualify him to enter his father's house. Thus, the father changed his clothing. To change his clothing is to redeem him. The father's clothing his son with the best robe and putting a ring on his finger and sandals on his feet signify God's redeeming.

Hebrews 13:12 says that we, the God-chosen people, were sanctified by the blood of Christ. Yes, the Spirit brought us back to God, but we were full of sins, so at that juncture, God applied Christ's redemption to us. Actually, Christ's redemption was accomplished already. This is signified by the fact that the robe for the prodigal son had already been made for him. The father told his slaves to bring out "the best robe" (Luke 15:22). *The* indicates a particular robe prepared for this particular purpose at this particular time. This shows that the redemption of Christ had already been prepared. When a sinner comes back to the Father through the Spirit's fine seeking, God the Father applies the redemption of Christ to him, and that is the sprinkling of the blood of Jesus Christ upon him (1 Pet. 1:2).

Now the sinner is not only back but also qualified to receive the top gift from God. This top gift is signified by the fattened calf. After the father put the best robe upon the returned prodigal, the father told the servants to kill the fattened calf for his son's supply and satisfaction. At the juncture we believed into Christ, God applied Christ's redemption upon us; at the same time God entered into us as the Spirit to regenerate us, to make us a new creation. But we need to realize that God's work to make us a new creation starts at our regeneration and is still going on in sanctification. From the time of our regeneration, the Triune God has continued His renewing work within us by sanctifying us dispositionally.

II. THE ESSENTIAL WORKS OF THE SPIRIT'S DISPOSITIONAL SANCTIFICATION

The final aspect of sanctification is the Spirit's dispositional sanctification. Our being sanctified through the blood of Christ was a positional matter. We were sinners in Adam, but Christ's redemption moved us and even removed us out of Adam into Christ (1 Cor. 1:30). This was a changing of our position. We were removed. To be redeemed means to be removed. When a sister goes shopping to buy some fruit, she removes the fruit from the market into her kitchen. This is a positional matter.

When the father clothed his son with the best robe, that was something outward and positional. But when he fed his prodigal son with the fattened calf, that was something inward and dispositional. Before a person goes to work, he dresses himself outwardly and eats something to supply him inwardly. His dressing is a positional matter, and his eating is a dispositional matter. The clothing changes his position and qualifies him to go to work. Then he needs something in his stomach to supply him from within. The blood of Christ changed our position to sanctify us. That is the positional aspect of God's sanctification. Then God regenerates us to make us a new creation, and this is the beginning of our dispositional sanctification by the Spirit. Our being made a new creation continues from regeneration throughout our entire Christian life by the Spirit's dispositional sanctification.

A. To Continue the Ongoing Work of the Believers' Regeneration

Dispositional sanctification is a continuation of the ongoing work of the believers' regeneration. Regeneration is a birth, and a birth is not a graduation. It is a beginning. Once someone is born, he needs to grow. Our birth is our regeneration, and our growing is our dispositional sanctification. God is now sanctifying what He has begotten. God has begotten us

(John 1:12-13), and now we need to grow. We all are children of God, but we are in different ages and stages in our spiritual growth. The Spirit continues to renew us by sanctifying us for our growth in life.

I would like to give an illustration to help us see the significance of the Spirit's dispositional sanctification. Suppose a brother speaks to his wife. Later, the sanctifying Spirit would ask him, "Was the way in which you talked to your wife holy?" Surely, this brother would repent and confess, "Lord, that was not holy. That was a common and natural person speaking, not a renewed one." The Spirit is sanctifying this brother in the way that he talks to his wife. While the sanctifying Spirit corrects this brother, He does something to infuse him by imparting more of the element of the Triune God into him to constitute him.

The Spirit does not just correct us but He constitutes us. To rebuke is outward, but to feed people with something is inward. Outward correction may cause us to change a little bit in our doings, in our actions, but inside we remain the same. The sanctification of the Spirit is not like this. The Spirit first outwardly corrects us and then inwardly supplies us with the divine element, infusing us with the riches of Christ and constituting us with Christ's riches as the constituents. The real sanctification is correcting plus constituting. I say this based upon my over sixty years of experience in the Lord.

Even in these recent days I have received much correction and much constitution from the sanctifying Spirit. A brother who does things according to his disposition may be enlightened by the Lord and pray, "Lord, forgive me. I am still doing things according to my natural disposition and not according to the Spirit." While this brother is being corrected, he is also being supplied and constituted with the riches of Christ. The Spirit sanctifies us not just by correcting us but by supplying us with His constituents, with His riches, with His divine element. The more we pray and confess to the Lord, the more we are supplied and transfused. This is the significance of the Spirit's dispositional sanctification.

B. To Carry Out the Renewing
of the Believers as God's New Creation

The Spirit sanctifies us dispositionally to carry out the renewing of the believers as God's new creation (Titus 3:5; Rom. 12:2b; 2 Cor. 4:16). Titus 3:5 speaks of the washing of regeneration and the renewing of the Holy Spirit. The renewing of the Spirit continues the washing of regeneration. In other words, renewing is a continuation of regeneration. When the Spirit sanctifies us, He not only corrects us but also renews us. To renew requires the addition of a new element. So the renewing is the continuation of God's new creation work, and *renewing* is a synonym for *sanctification*.

C. To Perform the Lord's
Transformation of the Believers

The dispositional sanctification of the Spirit is to perform the Lord's transformation of the believers (2 Cor. 3:18; Rom. 12:2b). Romans 12:2b says that we are to be transformed by renewing. Thus, renewing is a continuation of regeneration, and transformation is an issue of renewing. This shows that transformation is also related to sanctification. The dispositional sanctification of the Spirit is carried out by renewing, resulting in transformation. Both renewing and transformation are parts of the process of sanctification.

D. To Consummate
in the Believers' Glorification

In 1 Thessalonians 5:23, Paul expressed the desire for our whole being to be sanctified, that is, to be brought into glory in full. How much we are in the glory depends upon how much we have been sanctified. We are on the way of being brought into glory by the sanctifying work of the Spirit. The more we are sanctified, the more we enter into glory. Our being fully sanctified, not only in our spirit but also in our soul and even in our body, means our whole being has been reconstituted with the divine element. Our spirit, soul, and body will be reconstituted, sanctified wholly, and that will be our glorification.

Sanctification is the gradual process of glorification. The more we are sanctified, the more we are made holy and the more we feel that we are in the glory. When the Spirit corrects us, He supplies us and transfuses us with all the riches of Christ to sanctify us. Then we have the feeling that we are glorified. Thus, sanctification consummates in the believers' glorification.

E. To Complete God's Sonship in Choosing the Believers

Finally, the Spirit's dispositional sanctification is to complete God's sonship in choosing the believers. Ephesians 1:4-5 proves this. Sanctifying is sonizing. Sanctification is for God's making of sons. Sanctification issues in sonship, results in sonship. The sanctification which we enjoy is not only a change of our position but also a constitution of our disposition to sonize our entire being.

CHAPTER TWELVE

THE SPIRIT'S WORK ON AND IN
THE BELIEVERS

(4)

THE HOLDING LINE IN THE CARRYING OUT
OF THE DIVINE ECONOMY

Scripture Reading: Eph. 1:14; 4:30; 1 Pet. 1:2; Luke 15:8-10, 17-21; Heb. 13:12; 2 Cor. 5:17; John 1:12-13; Rom. 12:2b; Eph. 4:23; Gal. 6:15; 2 Cor. 4:16; 1 Cor. 3:12; 2 Cor. 3:18; Phil. 3:21; Rom. 8:23

OUTLINE

I. The divine sanctification is the holding line in the carrying out of the divine economy:
 A. Holding all of our spiritual experiences from our repentance to our glorification.
 B. Going through our regeneration, renewing, transformation, and conformation unto the redemption of our body—Eph. 1:14; 4:30.
 C. To sonize us divinely, making us sons of God that we may become the same as God in His life and in His nature (but not in His Godhead), so that we may be God's expression. Hence, God's sanctification is the divine sonizing.
II. The steps of the divine sanctification:
 A. The seeking sanctification—the initial sanctification—1 Pet. 1:2:
  1. Unto repentance—Luke 15:8-10.
  2. To bring us back to God—Luke 15:17-21.

B. The redeeming sanctification—the positional sanctification:
  1. By the blood of Christ—Heb. 13:12.
  2. To transfer us from Adam to Christ.
C. The regenerating sanctification—the beginning of the dispositional sanctification:
  1. Renewing us from our spirit—2 Cor. 5:17.
  2. To make us, the sinners, sons of God—John 1:12-13.
D. The renewing sanctification—the continuation of the dispositional sanctification:
  1. Renewing our soul from our mind through all the parts of our soul—Rom. 12:2b; Eph. 4:23.
  2. To make our soul a part of God's new creation—Gal. 6:15.
E. The transforming sanctification—the daily sanctification—2 Cor. 4:16:
  1. Reconstituting us with the element of Christ metabolically.
  2. To make us a new constitution as a part of the organic Body of Christ—1 Cor. 3:12.
F. The conforming sanctification—the shaping sanctification:
  1. Shaping us in the image of the glorious Christ—2 Cor. 3:18.
  2. To make us the expression of Christ.
G. The glorifying sanctification—the consummating sanctification:
  1. Redeeming our body by transfiguring it—Phil. 3:21.
  2. To make us Christ's expression in full in glory—Rom. 8:23.

In message eleven we pointed out that there are three aspects of the divine sanctification. Now we want to see seven steps of the divine sanctification. In this message we want to see the truth concerning sanctification from another angle. Sanctification, or being made holy, has been a great subject through the centuries in the study of the Bible. We are standing on the shoulders of many who have gone before us and have helped us to see more. They were our "ladders" and still are, so we have been unveiled to see some things which they never saw.

I. THE DIVINE SANCTIFICATION IS THE HOLDING LINE IN THE CARRYING OUT OF THE DIVINE ECONOMY

In this message we want to see that the divine sanctification is the holding line in the carrying out of the divine economy. It was not until the 1980s that I began to use the word *economy* frequently. Formerly, we used the word *plan* as a replacement for *economy*. God's economy is His plan, but the word *plan* does not mean as much as the word *economy*. *Economy* is a word anglicized from the Greek word *oikonomia*.

God's economy is the intention of His heart's desire, and God made this intention a purpose. This purpose became and still is God's economy. Sanctification is a great point in God's economy. It is the holding line in the carrying out of the divine economy. We need to see what the term *holding line* means. When a person goes fishing, he needs a line. That is the holding line for his fishing. The line holds his fish. In other words, the line directs his fishing. We say that sanctification is the holding line because every step of God's economy in His work with us is to make us holy.

God created the universe. Not one part of it was holy. Then God created man. Even before man's fall, he was not holy. In the whole universe, only One is holy, that is, God Himself. Regardless of how perfect and good someone is, this does not make him holy. The angels are perfect and good, but strictly speaking, they are not holy as God is. In order to be holy, you must have the holy essence. If something is called steel, it must have the essence of steel. Thus, if you are holy, you must have the holy essence, and the holy essence in the whole universe is God Himself.

The New Jerusalem is called the holy city (Rev. 21:2). It is built with gold, pearl, and precious stones on the gold (vv. 18-21). The pearls are for the gates, and the precious stones are for the wall with its foundations. These are built upon gold. Paul said in 1 Corinthians 3 that he laid Christ as the unique foundation and that now we must build upon this foundation. If we build with wood, grass, and stubble, we will suffer punishment. But if we build with gold, silver, and precious stones, we will be rewarded (vv. 11-15). Here Paul said that gold is a material.

Strictly speaking, however, gold is not the material *for* the building. Gold is the site of the New Jerusalem. The New Jerusalem is built on gold. When a person builds a house on a plot of land, the land is not the material *for* the building. The city proper of the New Jerusalem is gold. The street is gold. On this gold the gates are built. On this gold the foundations are laid and the wall is built. Gold signifies God in His divine nature. In the whole universe, only God is holy in nature.

Some may argue by saying that the angels are holy and that in the Old Testament there are God's holy people with the holy city. The temple was holy, and the gold was sanctified by the temple (Matt. 23:17). The priests were holy, the altar was holy, and the offerings were sanctified by the altar (v. 19). In this sense something that belongs to God can also be considered holy. Even the garments of the priests were made holy by being anointed. After being anointed they became holy because they became something for God and something belonging to God. But that is not the genuine holiness in nature. The tabernacle and the things related to it were not God Himself but were something belonging to God.

When we are speaking of sanctification in its highest sense in the New Testament, we are speaking about something not merely belonging to God but something which is God. Ephesians 1:4 and 5 speak of being holy unto sonship. We are chosen to be holy so that we can become God's sons. Since we are God's sons, born of God, we are not just belonging to

God. We are sons of God who have God's essence, God's life and nature.

The garments of the high priest belonged to God, but they did not have God's life and nature. Today, however, we are sons of God with the holy nature and the holy life of God Himself. We have the holy essence of God, so we are holy. But we were not created or born this way. We were created as common human beings, but we became fallen sinners, even God's enemies. But one day we were born of God, and this new birth revolutionized our essence.

Regeneration is a reconditioning. Regeneration reconditions us with something essential. This essential matter is God Himself. When He regenerated us, He was born into our being, so He became our essence, our nature and our life. Now we are holy, exactly as He is. He is gold, and we also are gold in nature. In this sense, only the ones who are born of God as His sons can be called holy people.

On the one hand, we are all holy, but our holiness is at various levels. One brother who has been in the church life for many years is more holy than a new one who has been recently regenerated. This new one's spirit is regenerated by God as the essence, but just a little part of his being is holy. His soul has not been touched much by the essence of God. But another brother may have the experience of being made holy for over forty years. His spirit has been sanctified, and his soul is greatly sanctified.

Our being made holy will be consummated at the redemption of our body, which is the transfiguration of our body. Thus, the sanctifying work of the Spirit first issues in our repentance and continues all the way to our glorification. In between our repentance and our glorification are regeneration, renewing, transformation, conformation, and the transfiguration of our body, which is the glorification of our entire being. This is the line of the divine sanctification to make us holy, so this line holds the carrying out of God's economy.

Today we all have been "hooked" by the line of the divine sanctification. We were in the "ocean" of humanity, but this line reached us, and we have been hooked. Our being hooked will be consummated when we are transfigured. Then the

line will be completed. A number of us were studying in
school when someone came and spoke something about
Christ to us. There was a "hook" hidden in this one's speaking, and a hook got into us. We were convicted and we
repented and believed. Then we were regenerated in order for
us to continue on the holding line of the divine sanctification.

The divine sanctification holds all of our spiritual experiences from our repentance to our glorification. It goes
through our regeneration, renewing, transformation, and conformation unto the redemption of our body (Eph. 1:14; 4:30).
Unto means "resulting in." The redemption of our body is the
consummation of the divine sanctification.

Such a sanctification is to "sonize" us divinely, making us
sons of God that we may become the same as God in His life
and in His nature (but not in His Godhead), so that we can be
God's expression. Hence, sanctification is the divine sonizing.
We are sons to our parents humanly, but we have been
sonized by regeneration divinely. We do not have and we
cannot have God's Godhead, but we do have God's life and
nature so that we may be God's expression. A son, in principle, is the expression of the father. God the Father sanctifies
us to sonize us, to make us His sons for His expression. In
regeneration we were sonized, but that sonizing is just a
start, an initiation. After being regenerated we need to grow
to reach maturity. We become mature when our soul is fully
sonized. Eventually, our body, which is still full of weakness,
sickness, lust, and sinfulness, will be transfigured, glorified
in full.

II. THE STEPS OF THE DIVINE SANCTIFICATION

A. The Seeking Sanctification— the Initial Sanctification

God in eternity past made an economy, and in that economy He decided to have many sons. After He created man,
man became fallen. Then God the Spirit came to sanctify man
(1 Pet. 1:2). We were lost in Adam, in sin, and in death. We
were in a heap of collapse, full of sin and death. But the Spirit
came to seek us out, and He found us. Then He convicted us.

Then He stirred up our spirit to repent. This was our initial sanctification unto repentance (Luke 15:8-10). This seeking sanctification resulted in our repentance to bring us back to God (vv. 17-21).

B. The Redeeming Sanctification—
the Positional Sanctification

The redeeming sanctification, the positional sanctification, is by the blood of Christ (Heb. 13:12) to transfer us from Adam to Christ. This changed the place where we were. This is the positional sanctification, having nothing to do with our disposition.

C. The Regenerating Sanctification—
the Beginning of the Dispositional Sanctification

Our regeneration is a kind of sanctification. Regeneration is the beginning of the dispositional sanctification to renew us from our spirit (2 Cor. 5:17). God renewed us from the very center of our being, which is our spirit. In God's salvation He first touches our spirit to regenerate it, that is, to renew it. This makes us, the sinners who were the enemies of God, sons of God (John 1:12-13).

D. The Renewing Sanctification—
the Continuation of
the Dispositional Sanctification

The renewing sanctification continues our dispositional sanctification by renewing our soul from our mind through all the parts of our soul (Rom. 12:2b; Eph. 4:23). Romans 12:2 says that we are to be transformed by the renewing of our mind, and the mind is the leading part of our soul. Our soul has three parts: the mind, emotion, and will.

Ephesians 4:23 speaks of our being renewed in the spirit of our mind. This means our regenerated spirit has entered into our mind to make us renewed entirely in our soul. This makes our soul a part of God's new creation (Gal. 6:15). Our spirit has become a part of God's new creation, but not our soul. Through the renewing, our soul will be made a part of God's new creation.

E. The Transforming Sanctification—
the Daily Sanctification

Second Corinthians 4:16 says that day by day our outer man, our old man, is being consumed, and our inner man, our new man, is being renewed. We should be renewed not merely day by day but also hour by hour and even minute by minute, continuously. Our entire environment, including the people around us, is the best instrument used by God to renew us. He is transforming us inwardly and metabolically with the divine element all the time.

The transforming sanctification is the daily sanctification which reconstitutes us with the element of Christ metabolically to make us a new constitution as a part of the organic Body of Christ (1 Cor. 3:12). This is a kind of reconstitution, to discharge the old and to add in the new replacement of the element of Christ. In order for us to be the living members of Christ, we need to be constituted with Christ's element to make us a new constitution for the building up of the Body of Christ.

F. The Conforming Sanctification—
the Shaping Sanctification

The conforming sanctification is the shaping sanctification to shape us in the image of the glorious Christ (2 Cor. 3:18). A fruit tree has the shaping principle of life within it. When a peach tree bears fruit, the fruit is shaped in the particular form of a peach. The regulating law of the peach life shapes the peach. In every life there is a regulating law. When the sanctifying Spirit sanctifies us, there is a shaping element to shape us into the image of the glorious Christ. This shaping makes us the expression of Christ. This is why we can manifest Christ. We express Christ because we have been shaped by the sanctifying Spirit.

G. The Glorifying Sanctification—
the Consummating Sanctification

The glorifying sanctification is the consummating sanctification, the completing sanctification to redeem our body by transfiguring it (Phil. 3:21). Our vile and fallen body will be redeemed from sickness, from weakness, from death, and from lust and sinfulness to make us Christ's expression in full and in glory (Rom. 8:23). At this point God's salvation and God's sanctification to carry out God's economy have reached the highest level. This is the revelation of the divine sanctification in seven steps.

The divine sanctification, from its beginning to its ending, is altogether the fine work of the consummated, compound, life-giving, and indwelling Spirit of Christ, the embodiment of the Triune God.

CHAPTER THIRTEEN

THE SPIRIT'S WORK ON AND IN THE BELIEVERS

(5)

THE RENEWING OF THE SANCTIFYING SPIRIT

Scripture Reading: Titus 3:5; Rom. 6:19, 22; 2 Cor. 5:17; Gal. 6:15; 2 Cor. 4:16-17; Rom. 12:2b; 2 Cor. 4:10; Rom. 8:18; Eph. 4:23; Col. 3:10

OUTLINE

I. The renewing is the continuation of the Spirit's sanctification—Titus 3:5:
   A. Regeneration is the initial step of the Spirit's dispositional sanctification in the believers.
   B. Renewing is the going on of this dispositional sanctification within the believers—Rom. 6:19, 22.
II. This is to consummate God's intention in making the believers His new creation—2 Cor. 5:17; Gal. 6:15.
III. This is a fine work carried out by the transformation of the sanctifying Spirit in the believers—2 Cor. 4:16-17:
   A. A daily process—Rom. 12:2b.
   B. A metabolic transformation.
   C. Through the consuming of our sinful body and its animating soul by the killing of the death of Christ—2 Cor. 4:10.
   D. Working out our glorification—2 Cor. 4:17; Rom. 8:18.
IV. It is accomplished in the spirit of our mind—Eph. 4:23.
V. It consummates in the maturity of our new man—Col. 3:10.

According to the teaching of the New Testament, God's salvation is altogether hinged on sanctification. We saw in the previous message that sanctification is the holding line in the carrying out of the divine economy and that this line begins from the seeking Spirit's sanctification. The Spirit's seeking us out is the initial work of the sanctifying Spirit. It is through sanctification that God carries out His economy.

God made an economy according to His desire. After He made this economy, He worked to carry it out. In this economy God purposely chose us to be holy, predestinating us unto sonship (Eph. 1:4-5). God's choosing is to make us holy unto sonship, to make us holy to be His sons. God wanted man to be sanctified unto His sonship, and He carries this out through His sanctification.

After His choosing, God created the universe with man as the center. But after His creation man became fallen, and God applied His anticipated redemption in the Old Testament. Then in the New Testament time, God came to be incarnated as a man, and this man is the God-man. God became a man to be our Shepherd. Luke 15 first tells us that the shepherd came (vv. 1-7). That indicates God's incarnation. The Shepherd came through the way of God becoming a man, so this shepherd is the God-man.

God not only became a man to shepherd us. In Luke 15 He is also the seeking woman, the woman who has lost a coin (vv. 8-10). Out of one hundred sheep, one became lost, so the shepherd went out to find it. The lost sheep which the shepherd went out to find was the lost coin which the woman sought. On the one hand, He is a God-man as the Shepherd to die for us on the cross. On the other hand, He is the woman, the Holy Spirit, to find the lost coin in a fine way by lighting a lamp and sweeping the house. This signifies the Spirit enlightening our heart and searching and cleansing our inward parts. Eventually, the lost coin was found by this woman. Christ, in His first aspect, is the Shepherd. Christ in His second aspect, is the Spirit (2 Cor. 3:17). He is a life-giving Spirit (1 Cor. 15:45b). In His incarnation He became the Shepherd. In His resurrection He became the Spirit. It is this Spirit who comes to find us.

The salvation of God begins with this finding. This finding is the initial sanctifying work of the Spirit. The sanctifying work of the Spirit continues in us until we are glorified. Thus, sanctification by the Triune God is the holding line of God's salvation. It is also the holding line of our spiritual experiences. Our first experience in our salvation was the seeking sanctification of the Spirit. The prodigal son in Luke 15 came to himself and repented because the seeking woman, typifying the Spirit, enlightened him and found him (vv. 17-20a). Our repentance came from the finding of the Spirit, and the finding of the Spirit is the Spirit's sanctification. The finding of the Spirit was the cause, and our repentance was the result. Our final experience of sanctification will be our glorification, the transfiguration and redemption of our vile body. We are redeemed first in our spirit, then in our soul, and finally in our body (Rom. 8:23b). The redemption of our body is the full sonship of God.

I. THE RENEWING IS THE CONTINUATION OF THE SPIRIT'S SANCTIFICATION

A. Regeneration Is the Initial Step of the Spirit's Dispositional Sanctification in the Believers

After our repentance, we believed and were regenerated. Regeneration is the initial step of the Spirit's dispositional sanctification in the believers. Sanctification follows regeneration and continues through our whole life until we reach the redemption of our body.

This sanctifying Spirit is the sealing Spirit (Eph. 1:13). He seals us unto the redemption of our body. Ephesians 4:30 says that we are "sealed unto the day of redemption." In my youth I thought the word *unto* meant "until." This would mean that the Spirit seals us *until* our body will be redeemed. This, however is a wrong teaching. *Unto* does not mean "until." *Unto* means "resulting in." The Spirit's sealing us *results in* the redemption of our body. *Until* refers to the matter of time. *Unto,* however, is a matter of result. The sealing of the Spirit results in the redemption of our body, which is the full sonship we will enter into with our glorification. Following regeneration is sanctification, and sanctification implies renewing, transformation, conformation, and glorification.

Renewing is a very fine work. Titus 3:5 shows how sanctification continues regeneration. This verse says that God saves us through the washing of regeneration and the renewing of the Holy Spirit. Regeneration is a great washing. We were created as the old man, and the old man became fallen. Even the best part of the old man is dirty and contaminated. It has been contaminated with sin, Satan, the world, and the flesh. So God came in to save us through regeneration, and this regeneration washes away the old creation with sin, Satan, the world, and the flesh.

B. Renewing Is the Going On
of This Dispositional Sanctification
within the Believers

This washing needs some continuation. Each morning we spend some time to wash ourselves thoroughly, but throughout the day we wash again and again. We wash our hands and face outwardly, and we wash our inward being by drinking water. Washing needs a continuation. Regeneration is a great washing, and our sanctification continues this washing. The first step of this continuation of our being sanctified is the renewing.

Renewing is the going on of the dispositional sanctification within the believers. Romans 6:19 and 22 prove that this sanctifying is going on. Sanctifying is a kind of renewing, and this renewing is going on every day and every moment through our entire Christian life. Verse 19 says that we should present our members "as slaves to righteousness unto sanctification." This means we should not let the members of our body do anything unrighteous. When we present the members of our body to righteousness, this results in sanctification. Verse 22 says that this sanctification leads us to eternal life. Righteousness, sanctification, and eternal life are covered in verses 19 and 22. How can we reach eternal life? We have to present our physical body in every way to

righteousness, and this results in sanctification. Then sanctification leads us to eternal life.

Early in the morning we need to pray, "Lord, thank You for
this day. I present myself as a burnt offering for Your satisfaction. Lord, keep me right the whole day." Then this will be
unto sanctification, and sanctification will lead you to eternal
life. Romans 6:19 and 22 show us a continual renewing, a continual sanctification. Sanctification is the general term,
and renewing is a specific term. In the sanctifying we have
the renewing every day.

II. THIS IS TO CONSUMMATE
GOD'S INTENTION IN MAKING
THE BELIEVERS HIS NEW CREATION

Second Corinthians 5:17 says, "So then if anyone is in
Christ, he is a new creation. The old things have passed
away; behold, they have become new." On the one hand, God
created the new creation. In God's salvation everything is
done once for all, but the application and continuation of
what has been done are needed. According to 2 Corinthians
5:17, in God's eyes we are a new creation already. But in our
experience we are not yet fully new. In our experience there is
a process.

In many things we are still old. The full-time training is to
help us not just in knowing things but in being renewed. All
the things in our environment should help us to be renewed.
Every kind of inward correction is a renewing. Every kind of
inward adjustment is a renewing. We need to be corrected and
adjusted.

Before leaving the room where we are working, we may
not return our chair to its original position under the desk or
return the books to their proper place on the shelf from which
we took them. Instead, we leave everything in a collapsed situation. This shows that we are short of renewing. When we
are corrected again and again, we are renewed again and
again. When we leave the room where we have been working,
the things there should not be in a collapse but should be
headed up in Christ. We need to be renewed in many small
things. Every correction is a renewing. This renewing is to

consummate God's intention in making the believers His new creation.

Many of us are too rough; we are not so fine. In 1935 I was staying with a co-worker in Shanghai. Because we did not have modern conveniences where we were staying, we had to go to the kitchen to get some water for washing. When I brought this water from the kitchen to my room, I had to pass by my co-worker's bed. When I passed by his bed, some drops of water spilled on his bed. That bothered me. I cleaned up this water, but I did not have the peace until I saw him and asked him to forgive me. This happened a number of times when we were staying together. Eventually he said, "The worst thing is to sin and not confess. The best is not to sin. To make mistakes and apologize is in between the worst and the best." I was disappointed and told the Lord, "Lord, I can never be the best. At the most I can only make mistakes and confess." That experience with that brother renewed me. If I had been careless, I could have spilled a little water on the brother's bed without being bothered. But if we are careless in our behavior, we will not be renewed. I am often corrected by the Lord within and renewed. I hope that we can learn to be so fine. We have to be trained both in truth and in life in this way.

Washing is a fine matter. In order to wash our hands properly, we have to wash them with soap in a fine way. The renewing in our experience is very fine. We must be washed and renewed finely. When we leave our desk, it should not be a mess, in a collapsed situation. We should clear up our desk, and it should be neat when we leave it. If our desk is a mess, that means we are still old; we need to be renewed. A renewed man would not live in such a way.

A number of years ago a brother went with me to the Philippines. One day some sisters cleaned this brother's room, and they were very troubled. His room was a mess. They saw one of his socks upon a cup on the desk. I talked to this brother and told him, "We are workers for the Lord. If you are such a person, how could you work for the Lord?" If we are careless in our living, we will also be careless and rough in the way that we study the Bible. This brother was

not a new man. A new man should be renewed, adjusted, corrected. Every mistake of ours belongs to our oldness. Why
are we wrong? Because we are old. A new man is not wrong.
A new man is always gentle, fine, and careful, especially in
his relationships with others.

Even in our own rooms, we should learn the lesson to put
everything in order. In order to experience the proper renewing for our growth in life, we must be very fine. Often after we
have a good time with the Lord in prayer, we become a very
fine person. Our time with the Lord causes us to be
restricted. If we did not pray, we would be loose and rough.
But after our prayer, we do not have the peace to do certain
things. This is according to our experience. How much we
have grown in the Lord's life is seen by how fine we are. If we
are too rough and too fast in doing things, that is not the new
man's living.

III. THIS IS A FINE WORK CARRIED OUT
BY THE TRANSFORMATION OF
THE SANCTIFYING SPIRIT IN THE BELIEVERS

Second Corinthians 4:16-17 says, "Therefore we do not lose
heart; but though our outer man is decaying, yet our inner
man is being renewed day by day. For our momentary light-
ness of affliction works out for us, more and more surpassingly,
an eternal weight of glory." The word *decaying* means "being
consumed." Our outer man is being consumed, but our inner
man is being renewed. God washes and renews our new man
by consuming our old man. The more we are consumed, the
more we should be renewed.

Regretfully, I have seen a number of saints being consumed without being renewed. I saw some brothers in
business make mistakes and lose much money. They suffered very much, but with them there was no growth in life.
Actually, every loss should, on the one hand, consume
our old man, and on the other hand, help to renew our inner
man. We should be washed through our sufferings. To be
washed is to be renewed, and to be renewed is to be transformed.

If we suffer because of our roommate, this should consume

our outward being so that our inner man can be renewed. You may be a proud person, so God may match you with an unsatisfactory roommate. Every day this roommate becomes an instrument to consume you. God matched you with such a person for your renewing. God also matches a brother with a certain wife to consume him so that his inner man can be renewed. If a brother is being renewed, regardless of how his wife behaves, he will not complain. This is the real growth in life.

A. A Daily Process

Romans 12:2b says that we need to be transformed by the renewing of the mind. This is a daily process, not a once-for-all matter. Our marriage life is part of this process for us to be transformed. Not one husband on this earth is perfect, and not one wife is completely satisfactory. In human terms we need to be adjusted. In spiritual terms we need to be renewed. With a renewed person, there is no complaining, because he believes in God's sovereignty. Things may be wrong, but the Lord will still bless us. As long as we have God's blessing, everything will turn out for our good, that is, for our transformation and eventual conformation (Rom. 8:28-29). We all have to learn the lesson to have ourselves daily and hourly processed by being consumed and renewed.

B. A Metabolic Transformation

Our being renewed issues in a metabolic transformation. In metabolism some new element replaces and discharges the old element. Our renewing is always a transformation. After a period of time, others should be able to see some renewing in us. This means that there is a new situation in us, in our living and in our behavior. We need to be renewed in all the details of our daily life.

C. Through the Consuming of
Our Sinful Body and Its Animating Soul
by the Killing of the Death of Christ

God has a purpose to consume our sinful body. If we are too comfortable and if everything is satisfactory to us, be assured that we will sin more. Being consumed restricts us from sinning. Our sinful body and its animating soul cooperate to do bad things. The soul is animating our body. Without the soul, the body is dead. The soul actually is the doer to animate the evil body. That is why God raises up circumstances to consume us. He may use our weakness and sickness to consume us.

This consuming is always realized and accepted by us through the killing of the death of Christ. Second Corinthians 4:10 speaks of our "always bearing about in the body the putting to death of Jesus." *The putting to death* is the killing. We need the killing of the death of Christ. We have a particular roommate because we need to be killed. A wife gets a particular husband because she needs to be killed. According to God's ordination, there is no divorce. We must take the putting to death of Jesus, the killing of Jesus. Then we will be renewed and transformed.

D. Working Out Our Glorification

The fine work carried out by the transformation of the sanctifying Spirit in us eventually works out our glorification (2 Cor. 4:17; Rom. 8:18). The extent to which we experience the Lord's glory depends on how much consuming we have gone through, how much we have suffered. Our sufferings mean a lot in God's purpose. All our sufferings are a help to our being glorified. Glorification is the result that comes out of our being consumed, our suffering. Romans 8:18 indicates that if we are going to be glorified, we have to suffer. To suffer is a condition, a spiritual term, God made with us. We have to pay the price of suffering for glorification.

This is all involved with the matter of renewing. Among God's people, the suffering ones are new. Those who are always enjoying riches, good health, and a wonderful situation are doing well in a material and physical way, but spiritually they are old. The suffering ones day after day become something else because they are being renewed. We must go through the killing, the putting to death, of Jesus so that we can enter into His resurrection.

IV. IT IS ACCOMPLISHED
IN THE SPIRIT OF OUR MIND

The renewing is accomplished in the spirit of our mind (Eph. 4:23). Our spirit is spreading into our mind. Romans 8:6 says that we need to set our mind on our spirit. Eventually, our spirit enters into our mind. Our spirit entering into our mind and our mind being set on the spirit are one thing. This means our mind and the spirit now are one. It is in such a spirit that we are renewed all day. All day we have to set our mind upon the spirit, and we have to have a strong spirit to invade our mind, to enter into our mind, so that our spirit and our mind are one. Then the spirit will take the lead, not the mind.

V. IT CONSUMMATES IN
THE MATURITY OF OUR NEW MAN

The renewing of the sanctifying Spirit consummates in the maturity of our new man. Colossians 3:10 says, "And have put on the new man, which is being renewed unto full knowledge according to the image of Him who created him." This is a very rich, all-inclusive word. On the one hand, we put on the new man; on the other hand, the new man is being renewed. This results in full knowledge according to the image of Him who created us. The new man was created in our spirit and is being renewed in our mind unto full knowledge according to the image of Christ. This renewing is according to the image of God, so it shapes us into the form of God. The renewing eventually will result in our conformation, causing us to have God's appearance.

CHAPTER FOURTEEN

THE SPIRIT'S WORK ON AND IN THE BELIEVERS

(6)

THE TRANSFORMING OF THE SANCTIFYING SPIRIT

Scripture Reading: Rom. 12:2b; 2 Cor. 4:16, 11; Phil. 3:10; 2 Cor. 3:18b; Phil. 3:12-14; Col. 3:10-11; Eph. 4:16

OUTLINE

I. The Spirit's transforming is the working out of the Spirit's renewing:
   A. Transforming is by renewing—Rom. 12:2b.
   B. Renewing is to deal with the oldness.
   C. Transforming is to bring forth Christ in newness.

II. Transforming is a metabolism:
   A. To bring in the new element—the riches of the Triune God embodied in Christ.
   B. To discharge the old element—the rotten things of Adam.

III. Transforming is a process through death and resurrection:
   A. Bringing our old man through the death of Christ—2 Cor. 4:16.
   B. Carrying on our new man in the resurrection of Christ—2 Cor. 4:11; Phil. 3:10.

IV. Through the Lord Spirit—2 Cor. 3:18b:
   A. Through the pneumatic Christ in resurrection.
   B. Through the life-giving Spirit as the reality of the resurrection of Christ.

V. For the growth and maturity of the seeking believers:

    A. By pursuing Christ—Phil. 3:12.

    B. By forgetting the things behind and stretching forward to the things before—Phil. 3:13.

    C. To reach the goal and gain the prize—the experienced Christ—Phil. 3:14.

VI. For the constitution of the members of the new man and the building up of the Body of Christ:

    A. For the constitution of the members of the new man—Col. 3:10-11.

    B. For the building up of the Body of Christ—Eph. 4:16.

In this message we come to the third step of the sanctifying Spirit. The first step is regeneration and the second step is renewing. Now we come to the transforming of the sanctifying Spirit.

The Bible is a whole revelation of God, unveiling God's economy. God in His economy desires to gain the Body of Christ to be the very organism of the Triune God. If we are going to understand regeneration, renewing, and transforming, we have to realize that all these steps are for God to carry out His economy for the producing of an organism.

For the carrying out of His economy, God created man, but man became fallen. Then God came in not only to redeem the fallen man but also to regenerate the rotten man. This regenerating means a lot. It means that Christ had to die on the cross to terminate the old, rotten man, to redeem the created man back to God, and to put this redeemed man into Christ. In Christ there is the process of death and resurrection throughout our Christian life. We are passing through death and resurrection all the time. This is God's ordained way. We have been redeemed back to God and put into Christ to go through a process of death and resurrection all the time.

This process begins with regeneration and continues through renewing and transforming until it reaches the goal, which is the last step of the sanctifying Spirit's work to transfigure our rotten, evil body (Phil. 3:21). Then we will have the consummating glorification. At that time there will be a Body in the universe before God. That will be the kingdom age with the New Jerusalem as its center. Eventually, after passing through the kingdom age, we will arrive at the fullness of the times (Eph. 1:10). The fullness of the times is the consummation of the ages. That will be the completion, the consummation, of God's carrying out of His economy in the new heaven and new earth with the New Jerusalem in eternity future. The transforming work of the sanctifying Spirit is for this goal.

We are regenerated and now we are being renewed day by day (2 Cor. 4:16). Transformation comes out of the renewing. Romans 12:2 says that we are transformed by the renewing. We were regenerated in our spirit. But we are still old in our soul and rotten in our body. So we need the further work of the transforming, sanctifying Spirit to renew our entire soul, our mind, emotion, and will. When our soul is fully renewed, we will arrive at our maturity and be prepared for our glorification, the transfiguration of our body.

This procedure, or process, implies the working of the death of Christ and the resurrection of Christ. Through the working of the death and resurrection of Christ, we are day by day renewed to be transformed. This goes on and on without ceasing from the day we are regenerated until the day we become matured. To be matured simply means we are ready to have our body transfigured that we may be glorified. Then God's work in us for the producing of His organism will be consummated. Now we know the proper position of transformation in the work of the sanctifying Spirit.

Transformation is a step on the way of God's process of us. In this transforming work, we pass through the death of Christ, which deals with and terminates all the matters of the old creation. Then we pass through the resurrection of Christ, which supplies us with all the riches of the element of Christ, who is the embodiment of the Triune God. Death takes away and discharges the old element, and resurrection supplies us with the new element, the riches of Christ, who is the embodiment of the Triune God. Now this element is constituted into our being. In this constitution is the mingling of the Triune God with His saved humanity. This is the Body of Christ, the organism of the processed Triune God.

Such a thing has been missed entirely by today's Christianity. Christianity's theology today is too traditional and objective. But the Scripture reveals to us a divine revelation, not a traditional theology. This divine revelation is very subjective to us. God wants to work Himself into us. In order to work God into us, Christ had to go through death to terminate the old creation and enter into resurrection to produce the new creation. The old element is discharged and the new element is supplied. This new element is Christ, the embodiment of the Triune God. The sanctifying Spirit transforms us by constituting the processed Triune God into us, the redeemed and regenerated humanity. The issue of this is the Body of Christ, the organism of the Triune God. All these things we are sharing here are part of our new culture. Hence, we need a new language full of new terminology.

I. THE SPIRIT'S TRANSFORMING IS THE WORKING OUT OF THE SPIRIT'S RENEWING

I purposely use the word *transforming* here, not the noun *transformation*. *Transformation* refers to a fact, whereas *transforming* indicates that something is going on.

According to Romans 12:2 transforming is by the renewing of our mind, including our emotion and will, that is, our entire soul. Renewing is to deal with our oldness. We need to be renewed because we are old, even stale. Transforming is to bring forth Christ in newness. To be made new you need some new element added into you through the resurrection of Christ. Something within us is going on positively and subjectively. That is the resurrection of Christ. Actually, that is the pneumatic Christ. The pneumatic Christ is the resurrecting Spirit. The resurrecting Spirit is the reality of Christ's resurrection, which is working within us all the time to bring in Christ. Thus, a new element is dispensed into us to renew us, and this results in transformation. Transformation is a further step of the sanctifying Spirit.

II. TRANSFORMING IS A METABOLISM

Transforming is a metabolism to bring in a new element. This element is the riches of the Triune God embodied in Christ, who today is the pneumatic Christ, the resurrecting Spirit. He is the new element. This transforming brings in the new element and discharges the old element—the rotten things of Adam. This is a metabolism to take away Adam and to replace Adam with Christ.

Transformation is a big replacement, but this does not mean that our being is taken away absolutely. It takes away only the fallen part of our being, and it keeps the part created and redeemed by God. Thus, the transforming of the sanctifying Spirit takes away the old, fallen part of our being and keeps our created, redeemed, and regenerated part for this part to grow, to be enlarged, and to increase until it will be matured in the processed Triune God. The new element is added into the God-created, redeemed, and regenerated part to increase that part with what God is. Then the divine element is mingled with the human element and constituted into the human element to make this constitution the organism of the Triune God. This organism is the Body of Christ.

III. TRANSFORMING IS A PROCESS THROUGH DEATH AND RESURRECTION

Transforming is a process bringing our old man through the death of Christ (2 Cor. 4:16) and carrying on our new man in the resurrection of Christ (2 Cor. 4:11; Phil. 3:10). In Philippians 3:10 Paul said that he desired to know the power of Christ's resurrection and to be conformed to the death of Christ. This means we need to be shaped, to be fashioned, by the death of Christ through the power of resurrection and with the element of resurrection.

The farmers who grow fruit trees know that the trees need fertilizer. If you do not fertilize the tree, the fruit will still come out but in a kind of poor condition. But if you add the proper amount of fertilizer, the fruit comes out in a richer way. That is a picture of transformation. The principle of transformation can be seen in God's creation. Without transformation, there is no growth in life. Growth in life means to pass through death and to enter into resurrection. In the spiritual realm, the death and resurrection are Christ's and the element is Christ Himself. His death and resurrection bring Him into us as the new element to transform us. In this transformation, there are the metabolism, the mingling, the constitution, and the organism, which is the Body of Christ.

IV. THROUGH THE LORD SPIRIT

The transforming is through the Lord Spirit (2 Cor. 3:18b). *The Lord Spirit* is a compound title. This expression confirms that the Lord Christ is the Spirit and the Spirit is the Lord Christ. The Lord Spirit is a compounded person. He has been compounded with all of the elements of Christ's person and work. Jesus was the complete God and the perfect man compounded together, so He was the compounding of divinity

mingled with humanity. That was His first step of being compounded. The second step was His passing through death and
resurrection. In this step He was compounded with His death
and its effectiveness and with His resurrection and its power.
In resurrection He became a life-giving Spirit (1 Cor. 15:45b),
and today He is the Lord Spirit.

Our being transformed is through the Lord Spirit, that is,
through the pneumatic Christ in resurrection and through
the life-giving Spirit as the reality of the resurrection of
Christ. Today this consummated, compounded Spirit is the
life-giving Spirit, and this compounded Spirit within us is the
resurrection. This means the resurrection of Christ lives in
us, and this living resurrection is the pneumatic Christ. *Pneumatic* is an adjective form of *pneuma*. *Pneuma* in Greek
means "the Spirit." The pneumatic Christ is the Christ who is
the Spirit.

V. FOR THE GROWTH AND MATURITY
OF THE SEEKING BELIEVERS

The transforming of the sanctifying Spirit is for the
growth and maturity of the seeking believers. This transpires
by our pursuing Christ (Phil. 3:12). Today the people in the
whole world are pursuing worldly pleasure and entertain-
ment, but we are here day by day pursuing Christ. Day and
night Christ is our goal. We pursue Christ by forgetting the
things behind and stretching forward to the things before
(Phil. 3:13). We even need to forget our experience of Christ in
the past. We should not stay with our past experiences. We
need to forget the many things behind us. One thing is before
us; that is Christ. We are forgetting all the things behind, and
we are stretching forward to possess the Christ before us.

We are pursuing Christ and stretching forward to reach
the goal and gain the prize—the experienced Christ (Phil.
3:14). I recently received a letter from the parents of two of
the full-time trainees, thanking me for training their sons.
Actually, however, I am not here training people. I am minis-
tering Christ to people and trying to take the lead to pursue
Christ. I only care for Christ.

VI. FOR THE CONSTITUTION OF
THE MEMBERS OF THE NEW MAN AND
THE BUILDING UP OF THE BODY OF CHRIST

We are the members of the corporate universal new man with Christ as the Head and with all the believers as His members. These members are constituted by being transformed. This transforming is a constituting work day by day in big things and in small things. In this constituting work, the embodiment of the Triune God, Christ, is being added and wrought into our being every day in all things. This is not only for the constituting of the members of the new man (Col. 3:10-11) but also for the building up of the Body of Christ (Eph. 4:16).

ABOUT THE AUTHOR

Witness Lee was born in 1905 in northern China and raised in a Christian family. At age 19 he was fully captured for Christ and immediately consecrated himself to preach the gospel for the rest of his life. Early in his service, he met Watchman Nee, a renowned preacher, teacher, and writer. Witness Lee labored together with Watchman Nee under his direction. In 1934 Watchman Nee entrusted Witness Lee with the responsibility for his publication operation, called the Shanghai Gospel Bookroom.

Prior to the Communist takeover in 1949, Witness Lee was sent by Watchman Nee and his other co-workers to Taiwan to ensure that the things delivered to them by the Lord would not be lost. Watchman Nee instructed Witness Lee to continue the former's publishing operation abroad as the Taiwan Gospel Bookroom, which has been publicly recognized as the publisher of Watchman Nee's works outside China. Witness Lee's work in Taiwan manifested the Lord's abundant blessing. From a mere 350 believers, newly fled from the mainland, the churches in Taiwan grew to 20,000 in five years.

In 1962 Witness Lee felt led of the Lord to come to the United States, settling in California. During his 35 years of service in the U.S., he ministered in weekly meetings and weekend conferences, delivering several thousand spoken messages. Much of his speaking has since been published as over 400 titles. Many of these have been translated into over fourteen languages. He gave his last public conference in February 1997 at the age of 91.

He leaves behind a prolific presentation of the truth in the Bible. His major work, *Life-study of the Bible,* comprises over 25,000 pages of commentary on every book of the Bible from the perspective of the believers' enjoyment and experience of God's divine life in Christ through the Holy Spirit. Witness Lee was the chief editor of a new translation of the New Testament into Chinese called the Recovery Version and directed the translation of the same into English. The Recovery Version also appears in a number of other languages. He provided an extensive body of footnotes, outlines, and spiritual cross references. A radio broadcast of his messages can be heard on Christian radio stations in the United States. In 1965 Witness Lee founded Living Stream Ministry, a non-profit corporation, located in Anaheim, California, which officially presents his and Watchman Nee's ministry.

Witness Lee's ministry emphasizes the experience of Christ as life and the practical oneness of the believers as the Body of Christ. Stressing the importance of attending to both these matters, he led the churches under his care to grow in Christian life and function. He was unbending in his conviction that God's goal is not narrow sectarianism but the Body of Christ. In time, believers began to meet simply as the church in their localities in response to this conviction. In recent years a number of new churches have been raised up in Russia and in many eastern European countries.

OTHER BOOKS PUBLISHED BY
Living Stream Ministry

Titles by Witness Lee:

Abraham—Called by God	978-0-7363-0359-0
The Experience of Life	978-0-87083-417-2
The Knowledge of Life	978-0-87083-419-6
The Tree of Life	978-0-87083-300-7
The Economy of God	978-0-87083-415-8
The Divine Economy	978-0-87083-268-0
God's New Testament Economy	978-0-87083-199-7
The World Situation and God's Move	978-0-87083-092-1
Christ vs. Religion	978-0-87083-010-5
The All-inclusive Christ	978-0-87083-020-4
Gospel Outlines	978-0-87083-039-6
Character	978-0-87083-322-9
The Secret of Experiencing Christ	978-0-87083-227-7
The Life and Way for the Practice of the Church Life	978-0-87083-785-2
The Basic Revelation in the Holy Scriptures	978-0-87083-105-8
The Crucial Revelation of Life in the Scriptures	978-0-87083-372-4
The Spirit with Our Spirit	978-0-87083-798-2
Christ as the Reality	978-0-87083-047-1
The Central Line of the Divine Revelation	978-0-87083-960-3
The Full Knowledge of the Word of God	978-0-87083-289-5
Watchman Nee—A Seer of the Divine Revelation ...	978-0-87083-625-1

Titles by Watchman Nee:

How to Study the Bible	978-0-7363-0407-8
God's Overcomers	978-0-7363-0433-7
The New Covenant	978-0-7363-0088-9
The Spiritual Man • 3 volumes	978-0-7363-0269-2
Authority and Submission	978-0-7363-0185-5
The Overcoming Life	978-1-57593-817-2
The Glorious Church	978-0-87083-745-6
The Prayer Ministry of the Church	978-0-87083-860-6
The Breaking of the Outer Man and the Release ...	978-1-57593-955-1
The Mystery of Christ	978-1-57593-954-4
The God of Abraham, Isaac, and Jacob	978-0-87083-932-0
The Song of Songs	978-0-87083-872-9
The Gospel of God • 2 volumes	978-1-57593-953-7
The Normal Christian Church Life	978-0-87083-027-3
The Character of the Lord's Worker	978-1-57593-322-1
The Normal Christian Faith	978-0-87083-748-7
Watchman Nee's Testimony	978-0-87083-051-8

Available at
Christian bookstores, or contact Living Stream Ministry
2431 W. La Palma Ave. • Anaheim, CA 92801
1-800-549-5164 • www.livingstream.com